on track ...
Talk Talk

every album, every song

Gary Steel

sonicbondpublishing.com

on track ...
Talk Talk

every album, every song

Gary Steel

sonicbondpublishing.com

Sonicbond Publishing Limited
www.sonicbondpublishing.co.uk
Email: info@sonicbondpublishing.co.uk

First Published in the United Kingdom 2023
First Published in the United States 2023

British Library Cataloguing in Publication Data:
A Catalogue record for this book is available from the British Library

Copyright Gary Steel 2023

ISBN 978-1-78952-284-6

Typeset in ITC Garamond Std & ITC Avant Garde Gothic
Printed and bound in England

Graphic design and typesetting: Full Moon Media

Follow us on social media:
Twitter: https://twitter.com/SonicbondP
Instagram: www.instagram.com/sonicbondpublishing_/
Facebook: www.facebook.com/SonicbondPublishing/

Linktree QR code:

Acknowledgements

Thanks to my dear friend David Cohen who introduced me to Talk Talk in 1986, to my wife Yoko, who uncomplainingly let me take on this project when I should probably have been taking care of the mortgage, and to Sonicbond publisher Stephen Lambe for waiting, and waiting, and waiting so patiently for my manuscript. Oh, and to the spirit of Eden.

'We are stardust, we are golden, and we've got
to get ourselves back to the garden'
Joni Mitchell

on track ...
Talk Talk

Contents

Introduction

Why would anyone attempt to write 50,000 words on a band whose entire lifespan was a mere ten years and whose recorded work over that time amounted to only one album every two years – a paltry five album's worth of original material?

It feels like an impossible conceit, especially given Talk Talk's rapid evolution into a kind of holy minimalism that valued silence over noise. Why chatter endlessly about a group that kept on subtracting layers until they simply ceased to exist?

The reason will seem obvious to both those who followed the group over its time on earth and the many who have discovered them subsequently through their profound influence on the more exploratory realms of rock music ever since their split in 1991.

Talk Talk are often credited with inspiring the likes of Radiohead and Elbow and Sigur Rós while unintentionally giving birth to post-rock, an impossible-to-define genre that denotes an adventurous aesthetic more than a specific style.

But perhaps it's the unsolvable mystery of the group's rapid evolution from early 1980s pop confection to a level of artistry seldom navigated in just a few years that continues to intrigue the fans who keep numerous Talk Talk social media pages buzzing.

Certainly, several authors have attempted to tell the group's story, most notably via the 2012 coffee table compendium *Spirit Of Talk Talk* and Ben Wardle's bulky 2022 Mark Hollis biography, *A Perfect Silence.* And yet, the group and the elusive crux of Hollis's secrets prove an impossible nut to crack.

While learning about the story and the personalities is fascinating, the reality is also sometimes disappointing. Hollis was an extremely elusive and ultimately private individual who rarely gave of himself in interviews. He never spoke about his private life, even to his closest music associates. It's somewhat inevitable that the more we learn about him also means the revelation of flaws that might devastate some dedicated fans.

While for many years an impenetrable wall of silence meant that we knew little about Hollis's personality or inter-group relationships, we now know, for instance, that he could be cruel and dismissive of others and loathe to appreciate – monetarily or gratuitously – the contributions of various musical collaborators.

While biography almost always disappoints as it reveals the human flaws in our god-like artists, I hope that my loving gaze at the group's oeuvre will place the art in perspective. It's the music that will remain as Talk Talk's gift to us, and the final three Talk Talk albums are destined to be discussed in depth – probably in much more detailed academic dissertations than this – for generations.

My hope is that this humble tome will also show that although Mark Hollis was the driving force and key artistic element of Talk Talk, the group's other members Lee Harris (drums), Paul Webb (bass) and de facto member and producer/writer/player Tim Friese-Greene were essential ingredients. Their subsequent work under names like 'O'Rang (Harris and Webb), Heligoland (Tim Friese-Green) and Rustin Man (Webb) proves that even divorced from the mothership, they were individually capable of substantial and sometimes astonishing artistic statements.

Listening again and again chronologically to the Talk Talk catalogue creates a quandary. It's a puzzle that can never be quite picked apart because the 1982 version of the group seems to bear almost no resemblance to the 1991 version or even the 1986 version. The evolution is so radical that it's akin to – and in many ways more extreme than – the rapid change of The Beatles from the four lovable moptops of 'I Wanna Hold Your Hand' to the psychedelic experimentation of 'Revolution Number 9' or Robert Wyatt's transformation from Soft Machine drummer to the bizarre otherworld of *Rock Bottom* or Tim Buckley's voyage from sensitive folk-rock pinup to the out-there screaming free jazz/rock improviser of *Starsailor*. Perhaps the obvious parallel is the way jazz legend Miles Davis evolved from the freneticism of bebop to 'the birth of the cool' to his reinvention in the turbulent improv-rock of his electric years in the early '70s. There are parallels in rock, but certainly nothing with quite the same trajectory during the 1980s – except for perhaps the art-pop progressions of Kate Bush and David Sylvian – and certainly nothing that resembles the specific dynamic of latter-day Talk Talk.

Talk Talk were perhaps the last rock band to exploit the big budgets of the major record labels to make art – hits be damned – and in the process, they created a whole new vocabulary of music. This book looks at how they carried off this canny strategy and why.

Baby Steps: Before Talk Talk

Despite the vast column inches devoted to Talk Talk in print, on fan websites and on social media groups, the biographical details of the group's motivating force, Mark Hollis, remain sketchy. In fact, even Ben Wardle's *A Perfect Silence* – a seemingly exhaustive 368-page biography – failed to turn up more than snippets of Mark's personal life, while details of his upbringing and young adulthood are still thin on the ground.

In this book, we'll keep the biographical details to a minimum, but it's worth spending a little time discussing the bizarre contrast between Mark's early musical experiences and where his aesthetic choices later led him.

Always a reluctant interviewee, Hollis would seldom answer questions about his early life and when he did, he was prone to tell fibs. We do know that he was born on 4 January 1955 in Tottenham, London, that he attended school at Muswell Hill, and he's said to have been a boy who had few friends and was happy with his own company. Brother Eddie Hollis, three years senior to Mark, would become an incredible catalyst and influence on his younger brother and introduce him – via his huge and idiosyncratic record collection – to the world of contemporary music. Eddie would also enable Mark's induction into the music scene, and provide unintentional subject material for Mark's songs via his unfortunate – and ultimately fatal – substance abuse.

Mark's spark may have been lit by punk, but the discovery in Eddie's collection of groups like King Crimson and artists like John Coltrane inspired him to want to take pop music in a different direction. Other acts that Mark turned onto through his brother included Jefferson Airplane, The Doors, Frank Zappa's Mothers Of Invention, and especially, LA flower power group Love.

We need to talk about Eddie, without whom Mark might have spent his life working as a laboratory technician. For years, Mark existed in Eddie's shadow. It was Eddie who was larger-than-life, and Mark, the quiet younger sibling few remember except in the shadow of his exuberant brother. Without Eddie's passion for music, Mark may well never have discovered his ability to forensically examine and isolate those elements of music he wanted to graft into his own work, and it was his discovery of key elements in the music he liked the best, way back in the mid-to-late 1970s, that stuck with him and finally flowered a decade later as Talk Talk became something beyond a mere pop act.

By 1975, Eddie Hollis was managing Eddie & The Hot Rods (no, he wasn't Eddie), who were part of the rough and ready Canvey Island scene along with Doctor Feelgood; a scene that, to many critics of the era, represented a refreshing back-to-basics, almost primitive approach to rock and roll to counter the musical frills of the progressive rock bands and the sartorial frills of the glam bands. Mark's first job in the music industry was as a roadie for Eddie & The Hot Rods, a group that, like Kilburn & The High Roads (featuring Ian Dury, later of The Blockheads), hinted at the punk explosion of the following year.

As unlikely as all this might seem when contrasted with the highly sophisticated work of Talk Talk, Mark championed authenticity in music and loved the energy of raw rock and roll. Although his best music would be light years from punk, Mark related strongly to its DIY attitude. And although he turned out to be a preternaturally talented singer, he remained essentially a musical dilettante throughout his career. Like former Roxy Music synth player Brian Eno, who admitted with some pride that he couldn't actually play an instrument, Mark would rely strongly on collaborators who could help turn his unique musical visions into reality. We'll return to this theme later on.

'Punk gave me the confidence, the opening', he would later state. 'Before that, music was too technical, it seemed to be reserved for the few. I had never considered playing. Finally, music belonged to everyone'. This statement is fascinating, given his predilection for the often complex and difficult-to-play music of heroes like Coltrane, Miles and rock groups like King Crimson. But while the proselytisers poked the borax at virtuosity, Mark was more prosaic. He'd found a way in, and he would spend the rest of his career figuring out how to 'paint' the music he wanted to hear.

Brother Ed co-wrote the first Eddie & The Hot Rods single, 'Writing On The Wall' (1976), which Hollis biographer Ben Wardle writes may have actually been penned by Mark, although we'll probably never know for sure. In 1975, Mark completed his A-Levels and began studying child psychology at the University Of Sussex, but he only lasted a year. That year, he also met his future wife and life companion, Felicity 'Flick' Costello. By 1976 he was convinced that a music career lay ahead, and he'd started roadying for Eddie & The Hot Rods, whose career would peak early with their only hit, 'Do Anything You Wanna Do' (1977).

In 1977, Flick supported Mark financially while he concentrated on songwriting and formed his first band, The Reaction, a trio. Several of the songs Mark forged during this time would be reborn with sleeker coats during Talk Talk's first years. At the same time, brother Ed had gained access to the Island label recording studio, having started Island label subsidiary Speedball (worryingly, named after a cocktail of heroin and cocaine that he loved) and he'd get random musicians in to jam and record together at the studio, including Island label heavyweights like Bob Marley and Robert Palmer. Mark was inevitably in the background at this time and witnessed his brother and others partying and partaking of drugs, but reputedly never indulged in mind-altering or addictive substances himself, apart from the odd toke on a funny cigarette.

During that same year, The Reaction played gigs in Sussex which were variously described as 'high energy' and 'psychedelic'. Ed had penned some of the lyrics for an early version of 'Talk Talk', which was supposedly adapted from a 1966 track by the group Music Machine (which had belatedly appeared on the critically acclaimed American garage rock compilation *Nuggets*). Later on, Mark changed the lyrics again so that it was 'anxiety' rather than 'society' that was bringing him down. 'Talk Talk Talk' (as it was known) was released late in 1977 by Beggars Banquet on a bargain-price compilation of new bands and artists, *Streets*, along with the likes of The Lurkers and John Cooper-Clarke. Produced by Ed and young engineer Steve Lillywhite, The Reaction's nascent version of 'Talk Talk' is a chrysalis of what it became and it doesn't really work. Even Mark's voice hasn't quite found its feet.

Island released The Reaction's only stand-alone single, 'I Can't Resist', in August 1978, having signed the group to a non-binding six-album deal. Like 'Talk Talk Talk Talk,' it was modelled on mid-1960s Californian garage rock, although the energy and speed are more reminiscent of punk acts of the time. While the musical style was sharply different from the direction Mark took in Talk Talk, a sampling of a lyric from the song reveals an emotional thread and an existential theme that would be central to his future songwriting: 'I must make sure to do the things I want to do/Life's just too short'.

The plug was eventually pulled on the group's deal with Island, however, possibly because the label had grown weary of Ed's drug rampages and generally unpredictable behaviour. And without their backing, The Reaction floundered and soon broke up. Their album was apparently near completion but has never seen the light of day. It is rumoured to have included a version of Love's '7 & 7 Is' and the masters are believed to still languish within the archives of Universal (that is, if they weren't destroyed in the infamous Universal Studios fire in 2008).

Although The Reaction were still limping along in the early part of 1979, Mark got to record nine demos for CBS under his own name that year, including future Talk Talk songs like 'Mirror Man', 'Renee', 'Have You Heard The News?' and 'Candy'. Listening to these tracks now, it's hard not to wonder why Mark wasn't instantly grabbed by a major label as a burgeoning talent, given the fact that his melancholic vocals were already clear and present, along with a number of demonstrably excellent songs. As several others have noted, 'Crying In The Rain' could almost be a song from some non-existent EP between *The Colour Of Spring* and *Spirit Of Eden*.

By the end of the year, however, his group had finally ceased to exist and Mark was said to be semi-destitute. Could it have been this tough time that gave Mark the conviction to take on the world with Talk Talk and, later, in taking two separate record companies for all they were worth?

In The Beginning: Talk Talk

Mark met Paul Webb and Lee Harris (who were still in their teens and seven years younger than Mark) in 1981 when they were in reggae band, Eskalator, with keyboard player Simon Brenner. Paul (bass) and Lee (drums) had known each other since they were kids, attended school together and were already performing together as an impressive rhythm section. Mark sat them down and played them lots of records they'd never heard, from his favourite LA hippy band, Love, to composers Satie and Delius to the cool jazz of Miles Davis and the prototypical garage-rock of The Seeds. Simon remembers getting stoned with Mark and how they listened to Bob Marley and King Crimson's epochal *In The Court Of The Crimson King*, which was one of his favourites. Simon's dad was a songwriter who had co-written songs like 'Born Free' and some Bond film music. Simon says that Mark loved crooners and the two of them briefly (and intriguingly) worked on some songs with his dad.

With Paul, Lee and Simon, Mark had found the core of Talk Talk Mk1. He just didn't know it yet. At that point, he was looking for a publishing contract as a songwriter and needed backing musicians to record demos of his songs. It was during the recording sessions that it became obvious the four musicians had coagulated into a group, even though, for a time, they remained nameless. Lee described the six months or so they spent in rehearsal coming up with songs as 'Crazy fun times, masses of energy and too skint to eat'. For a time, the group was known as 300 Cubs.

Ed Hollis was the fledgling group's manager at the beginning, but he was soon unceremoniously dropped for Keith Aspden, who was notorious for having arranged The Sex Pistols' infamous Queen's Jubilee boat party. Ed had given a tape of the fledgling group to Aspden's understudy, who had raved about Mark's voice. 'So we listened to it together', said Aspden, 'and it was obvious to both of us that here was a great writer who had a wonderful voice'. Songs on the tape included 'Renee', 'Talk Talk' and 'Magic Moments'. Ultimately, veteran producer Jimmy Miller (Rolling Stones, Traffic, Blind Faith) would be brought in to spruce up the demos, which would later be sold to EMI for Talk Talk B-sides.

Aspden soon left his job as an A&R guy at Island to concentrate on Talk Talk. He would stay with the group to the bitter end. After a period of matchmaking, EMI signed the group.

The Party's Over (1982)

Personnel:
Mark Hollis: vocals
Simon Brenner: keyboards
Lee Harris: drums
Paul Webb: bass guitar
Produced at Chipping North Studios by Colin Thurston.
Release date: July 1982.
Highest chart places: UK: 23, USA: 132
Running time: 36:47

Imagine if your first exposure to Talk Talk was *Spirit Of Eden* or *Laughing Stock* or even *The Colour Of Spring*. Imagine that you then started digging into Talk Talk's back catalogue, beginning with their 1982 debut, *The Party's Over*. The cover artwork certainly gives no indication that the sounds within are dramatically different to later discs, and the face with crying lips for eyes is in keeping with the conceptual continuity the group sought by keeping James Marsh on for every one of their album covers. The title is also in keeping with Mark's melancholy outlook, although it has yet to mature from the 'angry young man' take on melancholy into the deep rapture of his later work. Imagine if, having gazed at the cover and wondered about the title, you then put your stylus down on the platter and pumped up the stereo, and on came 'Talk Talk', and then its eight subsequent songs, all of them produced by Duran Duran man Colin Thurston with the same superficial gloss he gave to that superficial band. Yuck.

First impressions count, but it's worth diving down through that gloss because just under that top layer is a talented band and a decent record; just not one that has yet broken out of the tight strictures set for it by time and place and record company ambitions. And it's worth remembering that – even though Mark's idea of the group was vastly different to the reality of *The Party's Over* – he too was seething with ambition and knew that the EMI deal was his big chance.

When they signed with EMI, the group had played fewer than six live dates, and they were promptly sent off to support Duran Duran on tour, who were at their commercial peak between their two biggest albums, their 1981 self-titled debut and *Rio* (1982). It must have been challenging for Mark, who even then was a reticent performer who refused between-song chatter and blanched at looking directly at the audience. After all, nobody really cares about opening acts, and being painted as being somehow connected to a band he probably despised and had nothing in common with must have rankled.

Or maybe Mark and his colleagues didn't object in the first instance to the Duran Duran comparisons/connections, possibly seeing benefits in terms of audience exposure while knowing full well that they were from another

15

planet, musically and emotionally. Why else would they then allow EMI to foist Duran Duran's producer, Colin Thurston, onto their album debut? It's possible that Mark was just starstruck enough that Thurston had engineered David Bowie's *Heroes* album to think that he would bring out the best of Talk Talk rather than try and mould them into a kind of faux-Duran Duran. It's also possible that Mark was willing to go with the flow at this time, and that he secretly saw the linking of Talk Talk with the new romantic scene as a necessary bridge to cross in order to establish the group's name with the public at large.

For EMI's part, it seems that they were hell-bent on connecting the dots between the two groups (hey, they've both got double-banger names that repeat!) and it's likely that none of the Talk Talk members really understood the damaging implications of the Duran Duran comparisons.

Not, of course, that Duran Duran were awful, or anything. On their own terms, they're one of the most splendidly talented pop acts of the 1980s. The music press painted them as Thatcherites and Tories and aesthetically, they were exuberant proponents of a full-colour bursting out of monochrome new-wave traits into a lush, sexy and dazzling perspective. No wonder the kids went for them, as they did for the other so-called new romantic bands that told them it was okay to get up and dance and be happy.

On the one hand, the whole new romantic movement was a necessary reaction to the somewhat dour aesthetic of the post-punk groups, and let's not forget that even the most politically oriented new wave groups (The Gang Of Four) and the most inclined towards a depressive outlook (New Order, The Cure) found themselves in the new romantic domain by the early 1980s. An important part of the zeitgeist was the rediscovery of dance music and outrageous clothes and a sense of joie de vivre.

It's when you consider that fact that you understand just how stridently Talk Talk stood in opposition to all that, despite the fact that *The Party's Over* was dressed in the new romantic's best sonic costumery. The title says it all: the party is over before it has even started, folks.

Talk Talk couldn't have been more polar opposite to Duran Duran in their overall outlook and attitude and musical ambitions. There was certainly a massive chasm between how EMI saw Talk Talk and Mark's perception of his group, or at least, how he explained the group in interviews. A pointed example of this disconnect was the way EMI dressed the group in all-white suits for their first photo shoot and video. Mark thought of the group's real image as being closer to the rebel chic of The Doors, and in interviews, likened them to a jazz quartet. That seems disingenuous (or possibly sarcastic) but probably says a lot about what was cogitating in his mind but hadn't yet worked its way through to the actual music.

Recorded between December 1981 and January 1982, *The Party's Over* was released in July of that year to a collective yawn and a few bad reviews. It was an easy target for the UK music press, which predictably and unsurprisingly tarred and feathered Talk Talk with the Duran Duran brush. Critics accused the band of slavish imitation, too much reliance on technology, and having an airless sound, fake strings and clumping drums, and many swiftly consigned them to the new romantic pop dumpster. *New Musical Express*, however, gave it a refreshingly considered review, noting that there was 'a darker side; a gothic, almost celestial majesty'.

Forty-something years on from its release, it's now possible to hear it with fresh ears and dig beneath that shiny production to songs that, on closer inspection, have post-punk impetus not so far removed from the likes of Joy Division/New Order and Echo & The Bunnymen. Dig beneath the shiny production and the synth-dominated sound and it's obvious that underneath the time-capsuled gloss, there's a real band with real songs fighting to get out.

Regardless of the merits (or otherwise) of *The Party's Over*, it must have been a hugely exciting time for the band to have their album out on a major label and be sent on an all-expenses tour to America, playing to crowds of many thousands in support of Elvis Costello. The tour coincided with the 'Today' 12-inch single getting decent airtime on US radio, and they were able to headline a small number of their own shows there and even scored an appearance on *The Merv Griffin Show*. However, interviewed poolside in LA, they were described as hostile and Mark was already expressing dissatisfaction with the album, and hinting that the band were heading in a more 'organic' direction. Or perhaps the first-time travellers were just homesick?

Back in England, in any case, Talk Talk came thudding back down to earth at a disastrous, rain-sodden fundraiser for WOMAD with the angry crowd throwing mud and plastic bottles. Supporting a Genesis reunion with original singer Peter Gabriel, their quickly muddied Clockwork Orange-themed white suits and glossy pop were seen as a provocation by the hostile audience. This disastrous appearance was eventually followed up by the group's own headlining tour in the UK, in preparation for which they hired a Welsh cottage for three weeks (as you do). Ben Wardle's Hollis biography claims that the isolation of the setting pushed tensions within the band to breaking point and that, while Lee was discovering magic mushrooms growing on the hillside, Simon was being bullied by Mark, who couldn't get what he wanted from the keyboardist.

As an interim measure, Phil Ramocon – an experienced player with a jazz background who had performed with the likes of Jimmy Cliff – was brought in as an additional keyboardist for the tour: Brenner on synthesiser and Ramocon on piano. The bolstering of its onstage line-up didn't do anything for the reviews, however, which repeatedly made the assertion that Talk Talk had no stage presence and no personality. *New Musical Express* went a step further: 'His (Mark's) manner is that of a nervous accountant who by chance just happens to have stumbled onto a stage'.

While *The Party's Over* wasn't the smash hit EMI would have liked it to be, it hung around the UK top 100 for the last six months of 1982 and into 1983, and it was a big seller in tiny New Zealand where it went to Number eight on the charts. Two performances on *Top Of The Pops* failed to propel the singles or the album to stratospheric heights, possibly because Talk Talk simply didn't scrub up like real pop stars. The fact was that Mark's bird-like visage was nobody's idea of a teen idol, no matter how hard he tried to act the part.

Ultimately, *The Party's Over* contains a confusing mix of elements, with huge promise of leading somewhere great, but clearly, they're not there yet. As the main melodic and textural instrumentalist, such a big responsibility falls on Brenner's shoulders that it's not really fair, especially given that – as later Talk Talk records illustrate – keyboards are not to be the galvanising factor in their sound. But despite everything – despite the stylistic clash between Hollis's melancholic character and the bullish new romantic edifice the group are expected to fill – it's a pretty sophisticated debut album and one of the better albums of its type. Yes, it's date-stamped in a way that successive Talk Talk albums avoid, but there's a lot to like, nevertheless.

'Talk Talk' (Hollis, Hollis)

Even on the very first song on their very first album (and their second single, released in March 1982), Talk Talk is not quite like the others. The song that's also the name of the band is in many ways typical of early-to-mid-1980s synth-pop/new romantic/call it what you will, and you can instantly hear that they're part of the same firmament as labelmates Duran Duran, with whom they share producer Colin Thurston. Or are they? Mark's voice and the melancholy mood it generates is the point of difference, along with the angry cut and thrust of the song.

Where Duran and their contemporaries were relishing the high life in Thatcher's England, Hollis was berating people for talking too much and saying too little. There's plenty of fake energy and bluster in the music, but this is no celebration, even though it sounds like an anthem. In fact, where Duran and their fellow new romantic contingent wore their vivaciousness on their sleeves, there's no getting away from the fact that 'Talk Talk' is and was a bit of a downer. While the lyrics lack the wit of a bard like Elvis Costello, there's an undeniable connection in spite of Mark's attack on a lover who has proven deceitful and full of lies.

Coaxed into life by a lonesome drum machine before the swelling masses of Simon's keyboards and Lee's drums smash into the picture, it's a big and busy sound that's dominated by the clatter of drums and its dated synth sound. Simon's contributions are threefold: in the swelling 'organ' figure that provides the song's crescendo, the simplistic synthesizer arpeggio that would have been more at home with a band like Depeche Mode, and the brief acoustic piano interlude. It feels like Lee has been listening to Burundi percussion (or, at the very least, Adam & the Ants or Bow Wow Wow) and

Paul's plucked bass instantly evokes the fretless farts of Japan's Mick Karn.

Despite (or perhaps because of) its repetitive nature, 'Talk Talk' is an instant brain worm and, once heard, is hard to dispel, regardless of the fact that it's one of the more mundane melodies and rudimentary song structures that the band ever worked with.

Having written the song with the help of long-since-sacked brother Ed for The Reaction, it had kicked around for years and still retains vestiges of the garage/punk sound it boasted way back in 1978. In light of the restless inventiveness of their final three albums, it's hard to understand why the group included such an old song on their first album. Wasn't Mark already bored by it after four years? Regardless, in terms of its energy and spite, it's the perfect calling card and a great way to begin their first album.

'Talk Talk' would later be re-recorded with producer Rhett Davies in an attempt to better capture Mark's voice (he'd liked the way Davies had recorded Bryan Ferry's voice), but the result was underwhelming.

'It's So Serious' (Brenner, Harris, Hollis, Webb)

The thumping, galivanting drums and keys here could almost have come off an early Ultravox record and, lacking guitar, most of the orchestration falls to Simon's organ and synth. He makes an excellent stab at filling in the sound, but it's just not quite the right formula or contrast to Mark's voice. The chorus feels like it was written to a strict early '80s pop formula, while Mark's lyrics nag away at a theme that's only a few steps removed from 'Talk Talk', namely the lies and deceptions of someone and the consequential tears and sense of loss. 'It's So Serious' is a bit numbing in its over-abundant repetition, but it does have some pleasingly spooky, Gary Numan-like synth in the middle, and Lee and Paul give it a firm bottom end that's nicely emphasised by the 1997 remaster. Ironically, it took all four of them to write one of the weaker songs the group ever released.

'Today' (Brenner, Harris, Hollis, Webb)

It's shocking just how musically unsubtle Talk Talk could be at the beginning. Like 'Talk Talk', 'Today' features a strident, almost football chant chorus that's pure earworm, which provides a complete contrast to Mark's anguished vocal performance. Lee's drums (and 'claps') are as robotic, brash and dominating as his playing was subtle and engaging later on in the group's discography, and the song is filled out with more of those Numan-esque 'alien' synths and Paul again doing a squiggly Mick Karn-like bass thing.

'Today' is a minor classic of its era, however: a memorable pop song that, like all the best pop music, feels as though it almost wrote itself. The third single to be taken from *The Party's Over* was released on 12 July 1982 (the same day as the album) and its danceable beat and repetitive chorus captured the zeitgeist of that very synth-pop-oriented year. Eventually, it reached Number 14 on the UK charts, where it remained all summer. Its success even got them a coveted spot on *Top Of The Pops,* but once again, their televisual image lacked impact.

Cover illustrator James Marsh has commented that the bloody teardrop on the artwork of the single is to 'imply the heroin inference within the song', although a scan of the lyrics might leave the fan a little bemused. Where the words to 'Talk Talk' and 'It's So Serious' are straightforward, the verses of 'Today' feel like a puzzle, with lines like 'Happiness can often bleed/ Beggars lay among the sheep/Let me take the choice/The sermon pleads'. Like so many of Mark's later lyrics, guessing their specific meaning feels a little futile.

'The Party's Over' (Brenner, Harris, Hollis, Webb)

Mark is known for his less-than-joyful musical persona, but it's fascinating that even on the group's debut, he's already such a sad sack. I mean, with their first album, the party's hardly started, and he's telling us it's already over? But seriously, this would appear to feature a lyric about a relationship that's fractured under the strain of his own doubt. It's a mournful subject and a mournful song that goes on for an unfeasibly long time for a song on a pop album: six minutes and 12 seconds.

'The Party's Over' is comparatively low-key, starting with a gentle synth arpeggio and very synthetic-sounding drums, although it must be noted that Lee's drumming here and throughout the album is fantastic. He appears to be playing a natty combination of acoustic and electric drums and his playing is always solid and precise, and Lee and Paul mesh perfectly with each other in holding down the bottom end.

It's as though Talk Talk has got a bet each way between Ultravox synth-pop and Duran Duran's new romantic pop with just a dash of 12-inch remix 'groove' to give it ballast. (Although it probably doesn't need to be stated that there's very little funk here). The keyboards are very orchestral and emit more than a hint of the Asian cadence of the then-current UK group Japan, and near the end, Simon flourishes a choral effect.

Interestingly, it's already difficult to discern what Mark is singing about. That diction! Is it his teeth? His embouchure? Or was this a technique to disguise the words to make listeners concentrate on the sound and emotion rather than their interpretations of specific words? We'll probably never know, but Mark isn't the first to sing indecipherably. The obvious immediate predecessor is folk fusionist John Martyn, whose singing style bears some resemblance to Mark. Later, *New Musical Express* would write that 'Mark sounds like a man yawning with a mouthful of glue'. And while it's rather mean-spirited, they do have a point.

'Hate' (Brenner, Harris, Hollis, Webb)

Despite never actually turning into a song of quality and distinction, 'Hate' is an interesting hotchpotch. Mark's Joy Division influences are practically oozing out of him and the music, in many ways, echoes the precise moment that group evolved into New Order.

The band members once again offer up some soccer chants to counter lines like 'People crying/My illusion'. Meanwhile, the bass gets all bendy and the synth darts around like mad. Lee's drums are relentless and make the jungle-drum trend-makers at Bow Wow Wow and Adam & The Ants seem like rank amateurs.

Note the ecclesiastical references that abound on the last three Talk Talk albums are already cropping up on lines like 'The priest is losing faith' and 'stumbling into the flames', 'losing grace' and 'the devout prepare'. It appears, however, that by the end of the song, Mark has decided *not* to hate.

'Have You Heard The News?' (Hollis)

Another song that breaks the standard pop song length barrier at 5:07, 'Have You Heard The News' is the first song solely written by Mark, and one that appears to be based on an incident of some kind where a game turned into someone being badly hurt or dying.

Perhaps intentionally soporific to match the subject ('It's so hard to sleep at night'), it's a tired-sounding piece dominated by electric piano, synth strings and fretless bass.

A decent ballad with a soulful vocal. Had the song made it to a later album with a more organic arrangement, it might have carried more weight.

'Mirror Man' (Hollis)

The first Talk Talk single released in February 1982, 'Mirror Man' is a track in search of a sound; so much so that it's hard to understand the logic of a record company choosing it as the public's introduction to the group.

It feels like Talk Talk are gently exploring their options, experimenting within prescribed limitations. There are cheesy faux-orchestral synth lines and more bendy bass from Paul and time-stamped Syndrums and even what sounds like female backing singers on the wordless vocals of the chorus. Or did I imagine that?

In the context of the album, things flag a little coming straight after the sleepy 'Have You Heard The News?' although there's some entertainment value in counting the number of times they sing 'oh' during the chorus (17, by my reckoning).

Unusually, Mark's lyrics are conventionally descriptive and concern a couple who dress to impress. The man seeks to stay in line while 'she'll wear anything you can't recognise'.

'Another Word' (Webb)

The only solo compositional credit for bassist Paul Webb on any of the Talk Talk albums, this is a more straight-ahead, almost Duran-style number with clumpy drums and overtly decorative orchestral keyboards. The band members also get to sing some 'ooh's in the chorus.

The lyrics are somewhat ambiguous ('And when the riot comes/Keep your head and keep your loving charm/Living life is a glamour show'), but Mark sings them with characteristic passion.

Paul's New Order-style bass burbles away pleasingly and the song acquits itself as a 'near the end of album' track.

'Candy' (Hollis)

The album comes to an inconclusive ending with this slow, doom-laden piece that had been hanging around since The Reaction days and, once again, seems to be overtly influenced by Joy Division, even down to the beats, piano, synth and bass lines. But somehow, it's still cluttered.

Yet another song drenched in the pain of a soured relationship ('When I think about the times/That I laughed away the idea you'd cheat me'), there are a few genuinely odd lines that hint at someone who is really churning around his emotional angst and coming out the other side a bit disturbed. Hence, 'And I hope that I've kept you amused/To wipe that spit right off my boots'.

Perhaps the worst thing about *The Party's Over* isn't the Duran Duran-style production but the fact that the second side fades away and loses much of its traction after such a promising start.

It's My Life (1984)

Personnel:
Mark Hollis: vocals, acoustic guitar
Lee Harris: drums
Paul Webb: bass guitar, backing vocals
Tim Friese-Greene: synthesizer, piano, programming, drum machine
Ian Curnow: keyboards
Phil Ramocon: piano
Robbie McIntosh: guitar
Morris Pert: percussion
Henry Lowther: trumpet ('Renee' and 'Tomorrow Started')
Phil Spalding: bass
Produced at Wessex and Scorpio Studios by Tim Friese-Greene.
UK release date: February 1984.
Highest chart places: UK: 35, USA: 42
Running time: 43:13

What a difference 18 months can make. Although *It's My Life* is a transitional album, it's a vast improvement on *The Party's Over,* and the catalysing factor is undoubtedly Tim Friese-Greene, who had become central to the group's quickly evolving sound. Tim ended up not only producing and engineering the album but collaborating with Mark on several songs as well as contributing his keyboard and programming skills.

But how did this happen? Original keyboardist Simon Brenner had been kicked out of the band by the time the non-album track 'My Foolish Friend' (produced by Rhett Davies) was released in February 1983, backed with an early version of 'Call In The Nightboy'. Mark wanted a less synthetic-sounding sonic palette, and session pianist/keyboardist Phil Ramocon would prove to be one step on the way to achieving this.

Mark's brief writing partnership with Ramocon would prove typical of his approach for the rest of his brief career, the genius dilettante always searching for fellow travellers with the skills to enable his ideas to come to practical fruition. Ramocon says that Mark was searching for an emotional delicacy with a sense of space similar to that found on Miles Davis's *Sketches Of Spain* album, and wanted writing collaborators who 'knew how to manage material, augment melody and transcribe different song fragments into a coherent shape'.

Although keyboards – and specifically the much-despised synthesizer – would still play an important role on *It's My Life,* Mark's decision to start recruiting session players to fill out the sound with different textural elements would help to move the band away from the Duran Duran comparisons they had suffered the first time round. To this end, the album would be bolstered by the guitar skills of Robbie McIntosh, additional percussion by Morris Pert and the searing lines of trumpeter Henry Lowther.

McIntosh, who would feature on several Talk Talk albums and on tour with the band, is a guitarist with a sterling reputation, having played with a long line of A-list entertainers, including Paul McCartney, The Pretenders, Tears For Fears and latterly, Norah Jones. The late percussionist Morris Pert was a composer in his own right who had been a member of Stomu Yamashta's band as well as jazz rock group Brand X, and had done session work for Mike Oldfield, Kate Bush and many others. Jazz trumpeter Henry Lowther – who would work on all subsequent Talk Talk albums – has worked with Gil Evans, Charlie Watts, John Mayall and many more.

But obviously, the dominant new force in Talk Talk was Tim Friese-Greene, who would become second only to Mark in terms of guiding and defining what the group became. Tim had started out as a tape operator at Wessex Sound Studios and by the time he met Mark had worked with Thomas Dolby on the *Blinded By Science* EP and produced a few one-offs like The Nolans and Tight Fit. Mark and Tim obviously hit it off because their creative union would go on to produce three of the greatest albums of the era.

The basic tracks for *It's My Life* (originally pegged to be titled *Chameleon Hour*) were recorded in June and July of 1983 at Wessex Sound Studios with overdubs at the smaller Scorpio studio. It went way over budget and the band were reputedly 250,000 pounds in debt to EMI at this point. An indicator of Mark's increasingly experimental approach is that he talked about having chosen the lyrics using Brian Eno's Oblique Strategies, a set of cards that suggests a course of action to assist in creative situations. This cut-and-paste process suggests that expecting Mark's lyrics to make narrative sense or easily succumb to puzzle-busting might just be a waste of time.

While parts of *It's My Life* felt mired in the afterbirth of *My Party's Over*, there's half an album here that sounds like a prequel to the definitive mid-period statement/culmination that *The Colour Of Spring* would prove to be just a year later.

The album entered the UK charts at 35 on 19 February, the same day the Thompson Twins' *Into The Gap* entered at Number One. The following week, the Thompson Twins were still top dogs, while *It's My Life* had slipped out of the top 50. What does this mean? Maybe it means that Talk Talk weren't quite ready to roll out their first masterpiece.

'Dum Dum Girl' (Friese-Greene, Hollis)

From the first note, there's no mistaking it: this is the Talk Talk sound, or at least the culmination of what, on reflection, is their relatively brief dalliance with commercial pop. There's so much to like about this revamped version of the band. They're still recognisable from the group that made *The Party's Over*, but Tim's production and engineering are crystal clear and crisp, exposing the layers in their sonic splendour. And while there's a lot going on, the super-real clarity means that it never sounds cluttered.

'Dum Dum Girl' retains the pop smarts of the first album's better tracks along with the earworm characteristics, and the almost nursery-rhyme cadence-cum-playground taunt of its 'The DUM-dum-girl/The DUM-dum-girl' chorus repetition makes it immediately recognisable while also raising a big question mark in the listener's mind about its meaning. In fact, the lyrics really do feel like a puzzle with few clues, although Mark is quoted as saying that the song is about someone taking pity on a prostitute. Armed with that knowledge, it sort of makes sense.

The drum sound, the fretless bass and the shrieking synth are all still time-stamped to 1984, but the song's realisation – the skill with which the components are pieced together, and the overall dynamics are leagues ahead of anything prior. Almost as memorable as the 'dum-dum' lyric is the synth-on-South American-flute setting that echoes the chorus, while Morris Pert adds some appealing percussive effects.

'Dum Dum Girl' would be the third single lifted from the album, released in July 1984.

'Such A Shame' (Hollis)

Another song that instantly embeds itself in the cerebral cortex and just won't let go, there's electronic percussion and elephantine 3D sound effects like the intro to a wildlife documentary before the song finally kicks in.

Despite the odd beginning, it's such an obvious hit, with the band vocals echoing Hollis's brooding declamation of the title. There's lots of studio manipulation going on and a strange guitar solo that sounds like parts of it are played backwards; actually, a synthesizer mimicking a guitar, a tricky technique the group were to perfect with *The Colour Of Spring*.

Mark's impassioned, bravura, almost operatic performance gets you straight away, and it's a song that keeps its emotional intensity the whole way through. The orchestral synth lines have the melancholy heft of late-period Joy Division, and Paul's choppy bass isn't far removed from the sound being propagated by that group's Peter Hook in the post-Ian Curtis line-up of New Order.

Said to be inspired by Luke Reinhart's novel *The Dice Man*, in which the main character uses a roll of the dice to determine his actions on any particular day, the lyrics of 'Such A Shame' offer few clues. Like so many of Mark's best songs, the words are a mere adjunct to the sound and the emotion poured into the song.

At 5:35 'Such A Shame' is much longer than the accepted radio-friendly pop song, but nevertheless, it would be the first second single from the album, released in March 1984 as a double pack with a bonus single featuring the Jimmy Miller-produced 1981 demos of 'Talk Talk', 'Mirror Man' and 'Candy', and it was eventually a global smash.

Having conquered the Euro charts, the song received the absolute seal of approval with a James Last cover version on his *Non-Stop Dancing '85* album.

'Renée' (Hollis)

The longest track on *It's My Life* at an almost prog-like length of 6:22, 'Renée' is also one of its most low-key moments. This pre-Talk Talk composition is rendered here as a rather portentous, depressive ballad.

Perhaps best seen as a brief respite from the intensity of the first two tracks or an interlude between 'Such A Shame' and the album's clamorous title track, 'Renée' is most notable for the first – if tantalisingly brief – instance of Henry Lowther's unique, blaring trumpet sound; a close-up, microphone-saturated effect used extensively on the last two Talk Talk albums with both trumpets and harmonica.

Supposedly a rumination on a woman who is wasting herself on an older man, it begins slowly with a guitar figure and gentle percussion to go along with the rubber band bass and, before too long, liquid, floating synth. Weighed down by its own inertia, 'Renée' is the kind of tune that could stop a live performance dead and drain the enthusiasm out of an audience.

'It's My Life' (Friese-Greene, Hollis)

The first single released from the then-forthcoming album in January 1984, 'It's My Life' is another Talk Talk anthem with a chorus that sounds like it was tailor-made for the top 10. And posthumously, that would be the case. The song would prove to be their most successful track by a long shot, with over 100 million Spotify plays following on from the hugely successful (top ten) 2003 cover version by American band No Doubt.

But back in 1984, however, the song was only a minor hit, scraping into the bottom reaches of the major charts. Its success at the time was mostly in Europe, but that was enough to give the band the clout to do what they went on to do and the money to run away from the music biz. Every territory has its own perspective on Talk Talk, but this song turned them into superstars up there with Boy George and George Michael in countries like Germany, Italy, Spain and the Netherlands.

With its crying seagull synths and the very simple but vaporous, sonically distinctive two-note synth pattern, the song has already established its credentials in its unique intro. Its wiggly fretless bass, brisk drums and floating synth are presented in gloriously layered fashion. And on the chorus, a rich organ sound is used for the first (but definitely not last time!) to evoke a stately, deeply spiritual (or at least churchy) feeling. Add to that Mark's expressive vocal and a lyric that appears to be a soul-searching rumination about commitment to love and responsibility over and above freedom and career, and the song has us in the palm of its earnest hand.

Typically, the music press was dismissive, with lines like 'limp and whiney where it tries to be plaintive and yearning' being par for the course.

The single would be re-released to tie in with the compilation album *Natural History: The Very Best Of Talk Talk* in 1990, making it to number 13 on the UK charts, their best chart placing in the country of their collective birth.

And then, in 2003, American rock band No Doubt had a smash hit with their cover of the song, which was more popular than the original by miles, and no doubt (ha-ha) helped many new fans discover Talk Talk long after they were already kaput. Interestingly, No Doubt's Tom Dumont talks about 'a key change of a tritone from the verse to the pre-chorus that is theoretically the most dissonant and difficult key change to make, but they (Talk Talk) make it sound exciting and musical'.

'Tomorrow Started' (Hollis)

This slow, brooding number reinforces the idea that Mark (or perhaps Tim) held a candle for the second and final Joy Division album, and the orchestral synths and gentle pitter-patter of drums do nothing to destroy that illusion.

Regardless of the truth or otherwise of that observation, 'Tomorrow Started' is seemingly a fatalistic examination of the nature of destiny.

The instrumental intro takes a full 40 seconds before tantalising moments of silence – another technique the group used extensively later on – and into the song proper. Mark's vocal is especially keening, while McIntosh gives us a bit of rare guitar flagellation, using tones that emphasize the pain and suffering.

The colours and textures here (and elsewhere) are hugely improved by the extra instrumentation, with some gentle acoustic guitar, piano and a little more of Lowther's flayed trumpet towards the end.

A minor entry in the group's catalogue but worthy nevertheless, Mark described it to *Melody Maker* thusly: 'The intro reminds you of Erik Satie, the verse is maybe closer to Pharoah Sanders, and then the Marvin Gaye rhythm vibe comes in'. While that may have been a little fanciful (or satirical), there is a certain beauty to the way the piece trots along.

In Holland, EMI released live takes of this song and 'My Foolish Friend', which the audience preferred (apparently).

'The Last Time' (Curnow, Hollis)

Co-written with session keyboardist Ian Curnow (one of three keyboardists on *It's My Life*), this sounds immediately like they've beamed back to 1981, with the Spanish flourishes of its acoustic guitar and the chintzy synth sound. The plastic-sounding synth melody never quite gels and it's odd that it ever made it to the finished album song selection.

Curnow had been brought in to work on synth arrangements for the album for three months and was tasked as a kind of musical director 'for arrangements to fit Mark's vision', but obviously, the collaboration wasn't as creatively productive or as aesthetically well-meshed as the burgeoning relationship with Tim Friese-Greene.

Perhaps that's what Mark wanted to complement his words, with lines like: 'For the last time/Let the show begin/Bring on the clowns'. Is this his reaction to having to tour and perform each night?

It's certainly a rather ignominious addition to side two of the album and musically rather at odds with the rest. Phil Spalding plays the uncredited bass part on this track, as it called for a conventional bass part, and Paul exclusively played fretless bass.

'Call In The Night Boy' (Brenner, Hollis)

Just like *The Party's Over*, the album rather runs out of steam on the second side, or in this case, gets derailed by a couple of songs that feel like space-filling leftovers. First, an inferior and stylistically aberrant song by a session keyboardist, and now a track co-composed by their former keyboardist, Simon Brenner, who'd been sacked after the first album.

It's certainly big and bold with slamming drums and features the classic Talk Talk 'change' from major to minor keys, enabling a step into the anthemic chorus. While this propulsive, almost new wave track feels out of place on *It's My Life*, it's actually pretty good and makes a case for the unfortunate Brenner deserving more credit than he ended up getting.

There's a stealthy and mysterious feel to the verses and Phil Ramocon's piano solo is nicely demented. While it seems strange that the album omitted 'My Foolish Friend' while including this B-side, the fact that Talk Talk continued to perform the song up to their last tour suggests that they felt good about it.

'Does Caroline Know?' (Hollis)

Adding to the lengthening list of songs about Caroline (Neil Diamond's 'Sweet Caroline', The Beach Boys' 'Caroline, No', Matching Mole's 'O Caroline', Cocteau Twins' 'Looking Out For Caroline'...) 'Does Caroline Know?' refers specifically to this lineage in Mark's line: 'Does it matter if I can't say Caroline No?'

Beginning with the pitter-patter of congas, a chirpy synth figure and a burbling bass line, the song ticks over for a full minute before Mark emerges with a lyric seemingly about the breaking of promises. Nothing much happens during its 4:23 duration except that the gentle rhythm and swooning synths continue to do their thing.

It's a minor entry in the Talk Talk discography but a pleasant diversion, nevertheless.

'It's You' (Hollis)

Should Talk Talk have waited until they had enough new songs of the quality and distinction of 'Dum Dum Girl' and 'It's My Life' to fill a whole album? Probably. As it stands, they've got half of a very good album with some disparate loose ends tagged onto the second side, and they fail to find a cracker with which to make a good ending.

'It's You' once again sounds rather like a left-over from the first album with its strident new wave rhythm, in which the drums provide the accents and most of the dynamic. It's a dated approach and it feels like a cast-off from another band that's looking for a home – possibly a song Mark wrote back when he was looking at making it as a songwriter, rather than a writer/singer.

The lyrics appear to be blaming someone for not taking a stand for someone they clearly love, but who knows?

Above: Mark Hollis on stage in Utrecht in the Netherlands in March 1986. (*Rob Verhorst*)

Below: This shot of Talk Talk was used as publicity for *Spirit Of Eden* publicity, but was actually shot circa 1984. (*Kees Tabak*)

The Colour Of Spring (1986)

Personnel:
Mark Hollis: vocals, piano, Variophon, organ, Mellotron, electric guitar, melodica
Lee Harris: drums
Paul Webb: bass guitar, backing vocals
Tim Friese-Greene: piano, Kurzweil synthesizer, organ, Variophon, Mellotron
Ian Curnow: synthesizer
Martin Ditcham: percussion
Mark Feltham: harmonica
Alan Gorrie: electric bass
Robbie McIntosh: guitar, dobro
Morris Pert: percussion
Phil Reis: percussion
David Rhodes: guitar
David Roach: saxophone
Gaynor Sadler: harp
Danny Thompson: acoustic bass
Children from the school of Miss Speake: children's choir
Ambrosian Singers: choir
Produced at Battery Studios, Videosonics Studios, by Tim Friese-Greene.
UK release date: 17 February 1986.
Highest chart places: UK: 8, USA: 58
Running time: 45:40

How often does a band manage to squeeze out not one, not two, but three incredible, almost flawless, hugely influential albums one after the other? Talk Talk only made five studio albums in its lifetime, but three of those were masterpieces. The first of those was *The Colour Of Spring*, an album that was vastly different from the two subsequent masterpieces, *Spirit Of Eden* and *Laughing Stock,* both of which were kindred spirits and complemented each other, but which some fans found just too hard-going and experimental.

The Colour Of Spring is at once an artefact of the mid-1980s but also completely timeless. In other words, any musician and many knowledgeable music fans could date-stamp the album through its use of certain synthesisers and other gadgetry that was cutting-edge at the time. But miraculously, the album manages to rise above the technology that helped birth it at the time and it sits alone in the pantheon of classic albums as a thing unto itself.

Listening to the album nearly 40 years after its release, there's a freshness that never dissipates. Clearly, the group's collaboration with Tim had evolved at speed, and Mark's creative confidence resulted in a near-perfect collection of songs recorded with just the right elements to make them shine. *The Colour Of Spring* is the apex of Talk Talk's artistry as a commercial entity – regardless of the bizarre fact that EMI couldn't see it at the time – and one of the greatest achievements of any band, anytime.

While they would go on to make two more wildly innovative and influential albums in *Spirit Of Eden* and *Laughing Stock,* they were both defiantly uncommercial and required a new kind of listening. While *The Colour Of Spring* was a great album to listen to intently or have on in the background, *Spirit Of Eden* and *Laughing Stock* demanded that you dropped everything you were doing, got into the right mood, and gave your all to them. While there were fragments of pop sensibility about both of them, they were not pop records. *The Colour Of Spring*, however, covered all bases. It was accessible yet innovative; you could sing along to it, but if you gave it your full attention, the rampant experimentation within its grooves became apparent.

What Mark and his collaborators probably weren't aware of at the time, simply because they were so close to the project, was how the album would fit into the continuum of great British artistry; the fact that it's clearly in a lineage that runs all the way back to the more innovative late 1960s music of The Beatles and favourites of Mark's like Traffic, through to iconic/eccentric artists like Robert Wyatt and Kate Bush.

While Mark's vocals were a stylised take on soul, it's not Sam Cooke or Marvin Gaye we hear when he sings but an echo of blue-eyed English soul singers like Steve Winwood, whose music with Traffic was similarly restlessly innovative. While the songs on *The Colour Of Spring*, in part, conform to the self-imposed strictures of melodic pop/rock music, there's a world of musical adventure if you look through the cracks.

The extensive guest list is an extraordinary insight into the group's creative enterprise, as it contains a veritable alternative musical history. On a conventional album, session players are brought in simply to play parts that display their skill set, not their musical personality or history. But clearly, the session players on *The Colour Of Spring* can be described as guests or even collaborators, because their contributions, in many cases, carry with them whole micro-universes of English music history that invades the music like a good bacteria.

If you think this sounds fanciful, then take another look at that guest list. For starters, there's percussionist Martin Ditcham, whose embellishments are found on five tracks. Ditcham has a history that goes right back to the early 1970s as a founding member of that most English of experimental progressive rock/jazz groups, Henry Cow, but who went on to play with everyone from The Rolling Stones to Elton John. Then there's percussionist Morris Pert, who had played with the likes of Kate Bush, Mike Oldfield, Peter Gabriel and Peter Hammill of extreme progressive group Van der Graaf Generator. Acoustic bassist Danny Thompson's unique tones run through the more progressive strands of English folk fusion, from his group Pentangle through to sessions with the likes of Peter Gabriel, Kate Bush and John Martyn. And then there's Steve Winwood himself, one of Mark's all-time music heroes, who contributes his deliciously warm organ to three tracks.

And that's just a small sampling of the contributing musicians. When you add mainstays like David Rhodes and Robbie McIntosh, it becomes obvious that *The Colour Of Spring* isn't just a Talk Talk album but a kind of Talk Talk-PLUS that can't help shining a light on a uniquely British musical history with its own specific aesthetic.

There's also something about *The Colour Of Spring* that barely gets a mention elsewhere: that it's one of the best-sounding pop/rock records ever made. As a hi-fi reviewer, the album has perpetually been on my 'test record' list and never gets displaced. Audiophiles tend to gravitate to acoustic recordings for reasons of possibly mythical audio purity, the idea being that a live performance in a room with the best microphones and no overdubs and limited compression potentially allows for the maximum purity of sound. The more multi-tracks and overdubs there are along with the necessity for post-production, the more compressed and compromised the results tend to be. On top of that, pop and rock records are typically mastered for maximum loudness on radio or the best results on lower-bitrate streaming. Consequently, few pop or rock records sound that good when they're played on a high-quality, full-spectrum stereo system. *The Colour Of Spring* is a rare exception to the rule, its top end brilliantly crisp but not artificially bright, its bottom end full of heft and depth, its midrange dynamic and containing all the grain and resonance lacking on the average album.

The Colour Of Spring is almost flawless, but is there anything not to like about it? Well, there will always be a contingent of music fans who will find it aesthetically abhorrent. These are the music fans who only like the last two Talk Talk albums because they want it raw, ragged, even lo-fi, because somehow, they've equated the idea of lo-fi and raw with authenticity, and by the same token, equate sophistication with over-processed mush. And you know what? I can see their point. For all its utter brilliance, there's a slightly upper-middle class, comfortably Anglo-Saxon vibe that comes through its presentation. You hear the same thing on Kate Bush or Peter Gabriel or Genesis records. On some level, there's a profound lack of *funk*, but is that a bad thing? Of course not. Complaining that the intrinsic music aesthetic is too 'white' is just as silly as expecting a blues guitarist from America's deep south to incorporate the orchestral sensibilities of Delius. Unfortunately, there's a school of thought that intrinsic Englishness equals inauthenticity, and those music fans will go elsewhere for their thrills.

There's a case to be made that *The Colour Of Spring* is the last great progressive rock record, as well. Not that it's got any 20-minute, multi-part epics or gratuitous solos, but that it's somehow at one with that tradition, and especially the intricate studio craft of, say, 10cc or Pink Floyd circa *Dark Side Of The Moon*. Talk Talk sound like neither of those bands and Mark's deeply soulful, emotive vocals place them in a different universe, but their profound Englishness, along with the intricacy with which each song is constructed, forges a connection back to that time, and those bands.

Where the previous two albums had been simply collections of songs, and both had run out of steam by the second side of the vinyl, *The Colour Of Spring* is undeniably a complete work, from beginning to end, and every song is essential to the record, the running order perfectly chosen, and each song is of a piece: the perfect complement to every other song on the record. And although the compact disc was making serious inroads by early 1986, LP records still accounted for the large part of the market. In any case, while the album certainly used a degree of cutting-edge technology in its making, Mark's emphasis right up until his only solo album would be on the album as a two-sided artefact with roughly 40 minutes of playing time.

And then there's the cover. Right at the start, Mark made a significant and important decision not to picture the group on the album artwork, and instead, to use the artwork of James Marsh, whose paintings were plays on nature with an emphasis on birds and insects. Taking this approach in an era where groups were outdoing each other with crass makeup and costumery and ridiculous photoshoots and video clips must have seemed bizarre at the time, and is very much a throwback to the 1970s and the work of design companies like Hipgnosis. Even Yes didn't quite have the foresight to use Roger Dean's artwork on every single album cover, but Talk Talk stuck with James Marsh and the conceptual continuity of his artwork throughout their short timespan. The artwork on the first two albums seems clumsy and inarticulate compared to the gorgeous butterflies on the cover of *The Colour Of Spring*, however, where everything suddenly gelled. Even now, I find it hard to picture in my mind the covers of the first two Talk Talk albums, but the butterfly cover of *The Colour Of Spring* is unforgettable and instantly makes the listener want to experience the music within the cover.

But how did Talk Talk get to this astonishing place? *It's My Life* had done little for them in the UK, where they played to half-empty halls and continued to receive apathetic and sometimes downright derogatory notices from the music press and news media (*The Daily Express,* for instance, hilariously likened Mark's singing to music hall act Tommy Steele suffering a bad case of catarrh). The album and its resultant singles had been a hit throughout Europe and in other far-flung countries like New Zealand, however, as well as gaining a foothold in America, which must have given EMI the impetus to continue supporting the band.

But it was at this time that Mark also became disenchanted with the grind of promo tours and having to play second fiddle performing with the likes of Berlin and The Psychedelic Furs. The band – and Mark in particular – developed a reputation for being surly and unfriendly to other rock groups and musicians. Lee has even been quoted as saying: 'We were bastards... there were plenty of arguments and fights with other bands. No one seemed to like us and we quite liked that. We didn't get on with poseurs, all that superstar stuff'.

The fact that Tim had taken the better part of a year off to go travelling after finishing *It's My Life* while Mark and the boys had to get out and promote the album must have rankled.

Meanwhile, a new publishing deal was struck around this time, which made it clear that Talk Talk was Mark's band, and may have given him the impetus to dominate and dictate the terms with the next album. The new deal would make it clear that what Mark wanted, Mark got.

When the group reconvened to make *The Colour Of Spring* in January 1985, things would be very different in the studio, and their first masterpiece would take almost a year of six-day weeks to come to fruition. It would mark the first phase of Mark's determination to get everything exactly the way he wanted it, regardless of the fact that he often didn't know how to get it until it finally happened. This helps to explain the long gestation, the budget overruns and EMI's concerns, though apparently, they were hands-off in their approach.

There was an intermission in June for Mark to marry his partner of nearly ten years, Flick, and then on 27 July, they played at the Rock In Athens festival, where the camera is trained on Robbie McIntosh during the 'guitar' solo that's actually Ian Curnow's Roland Jupiter-8 synthesizer. Understandable, perhaps, as the synth solo does sound remarkably like someone shredding an electric guitar.

Tim – who had become inspired by Congolese soukous music – started piecing compositions together from the rhythms up, building the foundations on his Fairlight digital audio sampler, and then handing them over to the musicians for overdubbing: Ian Curnow for keyboard parts, Lee for drum parts. Tim had also hired Dennis Weinreich, an audio engineer he'd worked with previously. Weinreich is quoted as saying that the album was all analogue, no computers, just a drum machine with lots of valve recording equipment. He said that he used many odd compressor set-ups and that Tim was 'always taking the sound to another level. Just putting up the mic wouldn't do. We experimented with everything, mics, acoustics, playing techniques'.

Mark described Tim as more than just a member of the group: 'He's got to understand the music from the inside, and that only works if you've been involved in writing the songs. Technically, I'm very limited, so he has been able to kick my ideas into shape'.

Mark's buzzword was 'organic' and he wanted, as much as possible, to strip away the digital aspects. With his stated influences at that time being Miles Davis's work with Gil Evans as well as composers Delius and Bartok, there were a lot of potentially competing, but in actuality, complementary stylistic currents running through the album.

The Colour Of Spring would enter the UK charts at number eight on 23 February 2006 and would remain there for 20 weeks. It hit the number one spot in Holland and showed healthy chart figures in many countries around the world, selling around two million copies. Some would compare it to

Stevie Winwood or even Supertramp. In England, the music rags still couldn't quite get their heads around the album or understand Mark's defensive attitude, but internationally, *The Colour Of Spring* was enthusiastically embraced by critics and the public alike and has always been a firm fan favourite.

Curnow would score the gig as musical director of the subsequent tour, but *The Colour Of Spring* would be his last Talk Talk album appearance. *The Colour Of Spring* tour line-up comprised Mark, Paul, Lee, guitarist John Turnbull (from Ian Dury & The Blockheads), Rupert Black and Ian Curnow (keyboards), Phil Reis and Leroy Williams (both percussion) and Mark Feltham (harmonica). Mark, as always, retreated from any social activity apart from the odd beer, although legend has it that any new tour member was bullied into a marathon drinking initiation.

Mark reportedly grew increasingly disenchanted with having to do the same thing night after night and being away from his loved ones. As Tim noted, live performance was 'so unsuited to his personality, given that he hates revealing anything of his true self'. And now that they were having to play big gigs and festivals, Mark found that he had to self-medicate just to get through it all: 'I had to be drunk all the time. It wasn't a pleasure, it was a necessity. Without alcohol, I was unable to take the stage. When we started, it was the enthusiasm that drove me onstage, but that got lost. The routine, the repetition, killed it'. Everyone apparently knew that this would be his last tour.

The Colour Of Spring – together with all the other EMI albums – would be remastered and reissued in 1997, and again on vinyl in 2012 with the appellation 'remastered by Mark Hollis'.

'Happiness Is Easy' (Friese-Greene, Hollis)

The Colour Of Spring opens with one of the most unusual intros to any major pop/rock record: a crisp, thudding beat with a little percussive adornment that seems to go on and on but actually, is only 30 seconds long. Lee's big beats (filled out by percussionists Morris Pert, Martin Ditcham and Phil Reis) will throb and penetrate throughout the whole 6:30 of 'Happiness Is Easy', a song that rewrites the Talk Talk musical template along with what can be done with a pop song, but without completely abandoning their sound.

Even now, having listened to the song literally hundreds of times, I find it difficult to back off from it enough to dispassionately assess, as the emotions that run through it, together with the musical gestures that articulate and elevate those emotions, are so very strong.

First, there's Mark's plaintive voice, recorded really close up so that it feels like it's inside your head. Then, there's that beguiling and unexpected mix of elements, including the smooth, slightly haunting orchestration simulacrum, like a cut-off from the apocalyptic Mellotron on one of Mark's favourite albums, King Crimson's *In The Court Of The Crimson King*. Next, Danny Thompson's fabulous, fathomless acoustic bass with its woody resonance.

Not to forget that insistent strummed acoustic guitar, and the church/gospel organ by Mark's original musical hero, Steve Winwood. And lastly, one of the most extraordinary solos ever captured on vinyl, an unidentifiable instrument that sounds like a ghostly elephant apparition blowing a trunk-load of post-jazz expression. Is it an (uncredited) trumpet, altered in post-production in such a way as to give it almost extra-sensory dimensions? Or perhaps it's another of Tim's tricky 'sounds like' synth apparitions? He's listed as playing the Kurzweil synthesizer on this track, while Mark is credited with the Variophon, a gizmo that became inextricably linked with the last three Talk Talk albums. Whatever the case, it takes the song to another dimension.

The song's other genius move is to use an amateur children's choir to add a poignant sense of human fragility to a song that would appear to be an indictment of war propaganda. The slightly flat, rather dishevelled children's choir sings Sunday school lines like 'Little ships of Galilee/Standing on the sea' and 'Jesus, star that shines so bright', while Lee's drums insistently pound as if they're warning the kids that there's unavoidable adult hypocrisy and danger ahead.

The religious aspect can't go without comment. Mark has been quoted as saying that 'Happiness Is Easy' was about the holy wars, hence the reference to 'little ships of Galilee'. From this point on, Mark's lyrics will be scattered with Biblical references and imagery, leading to suggestions that he was secretly religious. In interviews, he denied the inference and it seems likely that the Christian imagery was simply a mechanism to convey meaning through the cultural references he grew up with. Popular music's favourite wordsmith, Bob Dylan, and other musical poets like Leonard Cohen, have often called upon such imagery in their work. And we shouldn't forget the song's title. Is happiness really easy? Of course not. It's one of the great ironic/sarcastic song titles.

Paul is missing entirely from this track, and the Average White Band's Alan Gorrie was employed to contribute whatever electric bass was required, though the drums and even the repeated lower octave notes on the piano add plenty of bass presence to the song.

'Happiness Is Easy' is one of those rare songs where the listener anticipates every little sprinkle of musical stardust and soaks it up with great pleasure, and like all the best music, you can listen to it endlessly and still be hearing new elements. Certainly, it wouldn't be quite the same without Robbie's judiciously placed acoustic guitar picking, or the restive piano during the verses, or ... or ...

If Talk Talk had never made another song, this alone would have made them a name to remember.

'I Don't Believe In You' (Friese-Greene, Hollis)

Beginning with a few notes plucked on a harp and a hint of the raucous Variophon (or is it?), the drums and shakers assert themselves, and a delicately strummed and picked guitar enters the picture, along with electric piano to build the basis of this slow, weary song. Smooth, melancholy orchestral synth accompanies Mark as he reveals that 'now the fun is over... I'm trying to find the path ahead'. For a change, the lyrics are relatively straightforward in what's clearly another song about a relationship that has faltered and died on broken promises.

Mark's vocal is sublime, soulful, and perfectly calibrated to squeeze the most out of every utterance. It's the same throughout every song on *The Colour Of Spring*: every syllable of every word is carefully articulated, not for literal clarity but for emotional heft and honesty. On 'I Don't Believe You', we get the picture: the character is trapped in a nightmare relationship that he's trying to get out of with some traces of self-respect left.

Every aspect of the music contributes to the overall impact: the clusters of Gaynor Sadler's harp blooming out occasionally to suggest memories of a better time, the way Lee's drums gather steam to match the anger in Mark's voice, and especially, the song's crowning achievement, the squalling 'guitar' solo, which of course turns out to be Ian Curnow freaking out on either a Prophet-5 or a Jupiter-8 synth connected to a fuzz pedal and through a guitar amp.

The story attached to the fake guitar solo is so odd that it sounds merely apocryphal, but Curnow insists that it's true: that Mark told him to play the solo like a rhesus monkey and had his hand gaffer-taped so he could only move two fingers and a thumb. It's an early indication of just how eccentric Mark's demands would become during the recording of *Spirit Of Eden* and *Laughing Stock*.

Another early indication of Mark's very specific requirements was the employment of a large brass section, all of which was deleted except for two tiny fragments: a trumpet player blowing spit at 0:46 and a squeak at 2:15!

'I Don't Believe You' (backed with 'Does Caroline Know?' from the group's 1986 Montreux Jazz Festival appearance) was the fourth and final single from the album, which failed to make much of a dent on the charts: not surprising given its rather downbeat nature.

'Life's What You Make It' (Friese-Greene, Hollis)
When Talk Talk delivered *The Colour Of Spring* to EMI, their record company insisted that there were no releasable singles on it, so Mark and Tim went away and wrote 'Life's What You Make It', which would be its first single and a hit in many territories. This was the last time that Mark would bend to record company demands, but its classic status suggests that EMI had a point. The group may not have liked being pushed into something as blatantly commercial as creating a hit single, but it's hard to imagine the album without this key song.

Once again, it's hard to know whether the title was straight from his heart, or an example of Mark's bitter disdain for his record company overlords and deep cynicism about pat statements. 'Life's What You Make It' sounds like it comes straight from a wellness motivational speech by some smarmy YouTube guru, but the song easily eclipses any such thoughts, and you quickly find yourself in its thrall.

Mark said in one interview that the song was inspired by *A Streetcar Named Desire*. 'There's a bird in that book who just spends her time living in the past. The song is a very simple idea. It lyrically deals with optimism'. So let's assume that the sentiment is sincere when he sings, 'Baby life's what you make it/Celebrate it', which is quite close to the kind of exhortation heard in American gospel.

Central to the song's magnetic grip is the drum figure that runs hypnotically throughout, and which Tim has admitted was loosely based on the percussive approach on the then-recent Kate Bush hit, 'Running Up That Hill' (a song that became a worldwide smash again in 2022 when it featured in Season Four of the Netflix fantasy-drama *Stranger Things,* which is set in the 1980s). Mark also likened the unchanging rhythm to that of one of his favourite 1970s bands, Can, and the relentless machine-like repetitions of their drummer, Jaki Liebezeit. Listen to the 1970 Can masterpiece *Tago Mago* (Mark's favourite) and the debt is clear.

This superficially simple but complexly layered song, buoyed up by the rhythm (and with Martin Ditcham's 'Christmas bell' percussion atop), featured a memorable guitar figure by David Rhodes, haunting organ and Mellotron by Tim and a perfectly simple, recurrent piano melody by Mark. Texturally rich, it just required Mark's anthemic vocal to turn it into a superior piece of earworm.

The B-side of the single was 'It's Getting Late In The Evening', which was recorded for the album but not used. A real fan favourite, it's often aligned with the more stark, minimal and chorus-free last two Talk Talk albums. (Ironically, the piano vamp in the song is said to be inspired by hearing The Doobie Brothers' 'What A Fool Believes' in a taxi!)

'April 5th' (Friese-Greene, Hollis)

'Let me breathe the colour of spring', Mark sings in 'April 5th', a piece that moves ever-so-closer to the awed reflections of *Spirit Of Eden*. While 'April 5th' captures that delicate bloom of life from winter into spring and luxuriates in its beauty, *Spirit Of Eden* takes us all the way back to ruminations more concerned with the very beginning of it all, in a Biblical sense. But 'April 5th' also captures something of the endless void that winter symbolises, but which could also be the end of an affair and the promise of something new in the future.

Once again, it's percussion that we hear before any other instruments or voice, in this case, a gentle echoed swishing and a tambourine. There's a sense of wonder in Mark's voice and the dreamscape made by organ, piano and Variophon, as well as David Roach's mellow saxophone, holds us in sweet suspension.

There's something non-denominationally religious about the way Mark sings, 'Come at winter's end/Gone is the pallor from a promise that's nature's gift' over the church-like organ (this time played by Mark) and the uplifting surge of the Variophon.

'Living In Another World' (Friese-Greene, Hollis)

While 'April 5th' is the perfect ending to the first side, the contrasting clamour and bombast of 'Living In Another World' makes for a perfect start to Side Two. It made for a perfect second single from the album, as well, and scraped onto numerous charts around the world without lighting them up.

While it's another great song, its flaw is that it's just a bit too busy: there's hardly any sonic space in which to breathe, with the collected might of most of the musicians all going for it at once. This makes it sound, in part, like it's almost a throwback to the better material on *It's My Life*.

As with most of the songs on *The Colour Of Spring*, the drums are mixed loud and crisp. There are acoustic and electric guitars, a smooth quilt of orchestral synth, and even before the first chorus, the sound is revving up with swelling organs (played by Steve Winwood) and Mark at his most declamatory. By the time the chorus comes around, everyone's going for it hammer and tongs, including good old Mark Feltham and his diatonic harmonica. In fact, he gets the only proper solo.

Thematically, it's yet another break-up song or at least a cry for help from someone who can't escape from the psychic space left by someone who has moved on. Mind you, in one TV interview, Mark insisted that the song was about the life of Jean-Paul Sartre, the father of existential philosophy. Who knows?

'Give It Up' (Friese-Greene, Hollis)

About as close as Mark ever gets to a motivational gospel number, 'Give It Up' showcases him as a superb blue-eyed soul stylist who, while clearly influenced by Steve Winwood, reached towards a much deeper expression of the form than any of his English musical ancestors or heroes.

The phrase 'give it up' by itself doesn't convey much, but the preceding lyrics give a guide to Mark's thought process and the need to overcome and get past inhibitions to get to the root of it all. It could be claimed that all of Talk Talk's latter music is a process of cleansing and rewriting a new reality, but this is the only time Mark's expression connects to the American gospel tradition.

Chosen as the third single from the album (it did get some chart action but did not worry the top of the pops), it features fruity organ (Tim), a strident bassline (Paul), a pleasant chordal melody on piano (Mark), and Mark's vocal exhortations make you want to stand up and chant in the Church Of Hollis!

Originally titled 'Having Sex With A Weird Bird' (!), the song also features Robbie McIntosh playing dobro over David Rhodes' guitar, and it's another masterfully-constructed piece with so much extra texture that it never palls.

'Chameleon Day' (Friese-Greene, Hollis)

Just Mark and Tim on board for this comparatively brief (3:20) track, on which they both play the Variophon – a wee gadget that produces a surprising variety of sounds but specializes in an imitation of various woodwinds.

Perhaps the closest they get on *The Colour Of Spring* to indicating where they would head next with *The Spirit Of Eden*, its hushed atmosphere can send shivers up the spine.

It starts with a prelude that sounds a lot like austere 20th-century classical music, with its palette of what sounds like trumpet, saxophone and miscellaneous reeds. Then Mark's introspective piano enters and his almost impossibly intimate vocal.

The lyrics are too minimalist to get a clear perspective on their meaning, but the way Mark emphasises the lines 'Breathe on me/Eclipse my mind/ It's in some kind of disarray' it seems that he's suffering indeterminate psychological distress.

'Time It's Time' (Friese-Greene, Hollis)

In true progressive rock fashion, the last track searches for and reaches some resolution to all the pain and confusion expressed previously. 'Time It's Time' segues from 'Chameleon Day' and the listener immediately feels a sense of relief, a lifting of the emotional weight.

Beginning with a gentle pitter-patter of percussion and one long note of synth orchestration against one of Mark's most sensitively crooning vocals, it's suggestive of hope. The song quickly builds to something of a crescendo, with crisp, whacking drums and a cheery bassline propelling it forward, along with a repetitive piano figure that carries with it the sense of a long journey to somewhere better. But the crowning achievement is the deployment of the Ambrosia Choir, voices which feel like they're ascending to the heavens. The catch is that while the choir are celestial, some of its members are singing at crosscurrents, a line that sounds almost evil, the kind of spooky effect used in films like *The Exorcist*.

But in yet another twist, this rather disturbing development is defused by the cheery recorders and wheezing harmonica that take over in the song's last, final resolve.

An ingenious piece and the perfect ending, 'Time It's Time' finds Mark still battling with the pain that he's been trapped with – in its various manifestations – throughout *The Colour Of Spring,* but now 'Time it's time to live/Time it's time to live through the pain'.

Taken as a whole, *The Colour Of Spring* feels like the working through of an intense and destructive personal relationship, but we know that Mark was married and the assumption was that his difficulties were in the way commerce intersected with art more than in the personal arena. We'll probably never know. Maybe he was drawing on the pain he experienced in a relationship prior to his marriage, or perhaps his words don't refer to a sexual partner at all. We do know that Mark liked that listeners would draw their own conclusions, interpret the words in their own way; and that the main objective was that the art, and the emotions, ring true. And they do.

EMI BOVEMA BV

BRONSTEEWEG 49, POSTBUS 139, 2100 AC HEEMSTEDE, HOLLAND
TELEFOON 023 - 23 14 14, TELEX 41257, TELEFAX 023-23 14 10

UITNODIGING

Hierbij bevestigen wij onze afspraak om op donderdag 18 augustus
om 19.00 uur in het 3-D theater "Omniversum" het nieuwe album
van Talk Talk **SPIRIT OF EDEN** te beluisteren.

Tijdens het beluisteren van **SPIRIT OF EDEN** zullen fragmenten
uit de op het "Omnimax Systeem" geschoten film "GENESIS"
vertoond worden.
Een unieke combinatie die U zeker niet mag missen.

Tevens nodigen wij U na de presentatie uit, om nog even een
hapje en een drankje te komen nuttigen in tuinpaviljoen
"Richter", dat achter het Omniversum gelegen is.

Adres: Omniversum
       President Kennedylaan 5
       Den Haag

Tot dan!

Promotie Internationaal

THE GREATEST MUSIC COMPANY IN THE WORLD
K.v.K. HAARLEM nr 40888 A MEMBER OF NVPI
A THORN EMI COMPANY

EMI 0288

Above: The Netherlands was the only territory to hold a launch for *Spirit Of Eden*
that met the band's approval. Here's an invitation to the event at a 3D 'Omniversum'
theatre. (*Albert Voorhoorst*)

TALK TALK......TALK TALK.....TALK TALK.....TALK TALK.....TALK TALK.....TALK TALK

By the time you receive this you will probably all be in possession of the new album, SPIRIT OF EDEN (released 12.9.88) and will know how brilliant it is. I must apologise for the incorrect release dates given last time - but they WERE correct at the time of writing and were only changed to enable simultaneous world-wide release.

There will only be one single from the album - I BELIEVE IN YOU - available 19th September and the video for it has been made and will be shown on Night Network. There definitely won't be any touring.

Talk Talk have been to Holland recently to air the album at a Press presentation at the Omnibus Theatre where a film called the Creation was shown on a wrap-around ceiling screeen, to an audience in laid-back seats! A similar presentation will be held in the USA soon.

I'm afraid the live video, recorded during the last tour at Hammersmith, will not now be released for sale, but hopefully you managed to catch it when it was shown a few months ago on late night TV.

Other snippets of information.....look out for October edition of Q Magazine and next weeks Melody Maker - both carry articles on the band - and pictures of Mark will his new short haircut.

Mark, Flick and Freddie are currently on holiday - taking a well earned rest.

Lee is now a proud father! His wife Jackie gave birth to a boy on 10th August and he's been named Daniel - Congratulations to them all.

If any overseas fans have problems getting hold of Q magazine, let me know and I'll try to get some - or if not, I'll at least photo copy the interview for you.

Around January, Mark will start work on the NEXT album!

That's all the news for now I'm afraid.

Till next time,

Take care,

Vivienne

Above and right: Two letters addressed to members of the Talk Talk fanclub. They were the first in anticipation of the imminent release of *Spirit Of Eden*, and the second inevitably expressing the frustration of running a fanclub for a band who have become insular and completely artistically driven. (*Albert Voorhoorst*)

19 JUNE 1990

Hi,

I'm sorry its been such a long time since I wrote, but I think you know
that I have a very demanding full time job and this is only a sideline.
Plus of course there hasn't been a lot to tell and I've been as much out
of touch as you have.

In view of the re-release of IT'S MY LIFE and the compilation album/video
I thought I'd better do some catching up, so I called Keith, their manager.

Since the release of SPIRIT OF EDEN they've been caught up in a legal
battle with EMI and it took them a year to get it settled. They fortunately
won the case and were able to sign to Phonogram. It is of course EMI
who have released THE VERY BEST OF TALK TALK - this seems to be quite a
usual event when a band leaves a label.

Anyway, the Court case gave Mark plenty of time to put some ideas together
and so now it'll only be a short time before they've got all their songs
written. They hope to start recording in August and be finished by December.

It's obviously far too early to have titles or release dates or even any
idea whether they'll tour or not - but I wouldn't mind betting we'll see
them on the road next summer.

Mark has been busy in other areas too - he's become a Dad for the second
time! It was another boy - to be called Charlie. For those of you who don't
know, the first boy is called Fred. So Congratulations to them all.

Well, that's the basic news - if any of you would like to ask specific
questions I'll be glad to find out the answers for you if I can.

As you know, we haven't asked for any renewal fees because it's practically
impossible to run a fan club for a band like Talk Talk - however I do know
how important it is for you to receive information. Therefore all I ask is
that you send Stamped, addressed envelopes - two would be ideal, and for
those of you overseas if you could send International Reply Coupons, I'll
keep you as up to date as I can.

Bye for now,

Vivienne

1 KENWOOD CLOSE, SIPSON VILLAGE, WEST DRAYTON, MIDDLESEX UB7 OJY - ENGLAND.

Spirit Of Eden (1988)

Personnel:
Mark Hollis: vocals, piano, organ, guitar, melodica, Variophon
Lee Harris: drums
Paul Webb: bass guitar
Tim Friese-Greene: harmonium, piano, organ, guitar
Martin Ditcham: percussion
Robbie McIntosh: guitar, dobro
Mark Feltham: harmonica
Simon Edwards: bass
Danny Thompson: acoustic bass
Henry Lowther: trumpet
Nigel Kennedy: violin
Hugh Davies: shozygs
Andrew Stowell: bassoon
Michael Jeans: oboe
Andrew Marriner: clarinet
Christopher Hooker: cor anglais
Choir of Chelmsford Cathedral
Phill Brown: bowed guitar
Produced at Wessex Studios by Tim Friese-Greene.
Engineered by Phill Brown.
UK release date: 16 September 1988.
Highest chart places: UK: 19
Running time: 41:30

It's hard not to have some sympathy for the group's record company, EMI, which showed faith in Talk Talk, nurturing them and putting up with hugely extended recording sessions and blown budgets. The success of *The Colour Of Spring* had shown that their commitment to the group was justified. Having forked out a huge advance for its follow-up, they must have expected a sequel, rather than a completely radical make-over with no radio-playable songs and, therefore, no commercial potential.

Mark and the band had their artistic sensibilities deeply attached to the 1970s, where for a time, groups like Led Zeppelin and Pink Floyd could do what they wanted with little interest in hit singles. For those 1970s icons, it was all about the album as complete artistic statements, but times had changed. Hit singles had once again become all-important in the 1980s and record companies expected bands to capitalise on their success, not completely change their formula.

In the much leaner industry environment of the 21st century, it's hard to imagine that a record company could have been as hands-off as EMI were during the gestation of *Spirit Of Eden*. In fact, it seems bizarre that, having spent so much on it, their record company didn't get to even hear the results until it was all in the bag.

It's easy to paint the record company as the villains in this story, but given the template – it is called the music *industry*, after all – where commercial, not artistic success is the goal, it's really rather astounding that art ever completely wins the day. From a business point of view, it's hard to avoid deducing that Mark pulled a swift one on the record company by keeping them in the dark and then delivering a product that was never going to be a box office winner. But there's no arguing about *Spirit Of Eden* as an artistic statement. And 35-odd years on from its creation, it's this towering work of art that matters, not the trifling matter of the unsavoury business matters that surrounded it.

One unavoidable and salient fact, however, is that *Spirit Of Eden* and its spiritual sequel, *Laughing Stock,* were perhaps the last times the record industry pumped real money into experimental music. In the wake of these two albums, a whole scene would grow and thrive, but it became incredibly rare to have the backing of a major record company, and independent companies couldn't afford the exorbitant advances or have the cash for year-long stints in expensive recording studios.

Time and the slavish imitation by dozens of Talk Talk-influenced bands may have blunted its impact a little, but when approached in the right way, *Spirit Of Eden* is still almost as shockingly fresh as it was on the day of its release, 12 September 1988. The first thing you notice is the absence of any obviously synthetic instruments. The second thing you notice is how very quiet it is, and how the loud bits stand out in stark contrast, making it an album of extreme dynamics.

While *The Colour Of Spring* had something of the slightly bourgeoise sound of Peter Gabriel in his post-progressive rock guise but thematically played out like a 1970s record in the orbit of progressive rock, *Spirit Of Eden* is even closer to that much-derided genre in the shocking volume blasts and the contrasts between instruments that seldom play well together. Progressive rock had innovated the studio-only fabrication of delicate acoustic guitars and flutes dancing nimbly with loud drums and electric instruments at a time when live reproduction of acoustic elements wasn't up to the task. Talk Talk never intentionally built tricky time signatures or impossibly fast keyboard passages into their compositions, but they were exceptionally 'prog' by the above definition. Oh, and the length of the songs: the opening track, 'The Rainbow', at 9:05, and the opening side coming across like one long composition but actually three linked tracks. In fact, five of the six tracks boast a running time in excess of six minutes. How 'prog' is that?

It's hard to know where to start with an album that almost always makes it into critics' lists of all-time favourite albums and has already had reams of purple prose written about it. I've intentionally ignored all that in an attempt to give my singular perspective rather than deliver a composite of others' opinions.

For me, *The Colour Of Spring* is the most listenable Talk Talk album, and it's the one I can easily digest regardless of my mood at the time. *Spirit Of*

Eden and *Laughing Stock,* on the other hand, are almost interchangeable in a sense, in that they're albums for special occasions; they demand your full attention, that you play them as a kind of sacrament, and you set the scene and play them as loud as your senses will allow. If anything, *Spirit Of Eden* is the more accessible of the two, because the recording feels like it has more air around it and there's less guitar dissonance.

Spirit Of Eden is noticeably less 'hi-fi' than its predecessor and its occasional sonic abrasiveness is aesthetically closer to the many so-called post-rock bands it influenced. There are songs here, for sure, and beautiful ones at that, but it would be stretching things to call this 'pop music' or even rock music because there's little obvious sign of either. On the other hand, the smooth jazz of Gil Evans-era Miles Davis is present, as are elements of 20th-century classical music and even a mutant blues in the extraordinary diatonic blues harp wailings of Mark Feltham. There are also elements of folk and church music, and as odd as all that seems, these threads flow together perfectly.

After the last-ever Talk Talk live dates, Mark was ready for change, both in his home life and music. With Flick expecting their first child, he bought a Victorian country house in a small village, Stanningford, and moved away from London. After a sizeable break, work on the album began in May 1987, and it was recorded in Wessex Studio – a converted church in West London – over the next nine months in sessions that have, over time, only grown in mystique. It started with Mark wanting to use only pre-1970 equipment (the one concession to digital technology being the 32-track Mitsubishi desk it was recorded on) and evolved into one of the strangest sessions in the history of recorded music. Paul brought in sound-triggered lighting around his drums and installed an oil-wheel projector, which beamed psychedelic images around the otherwise completely dark studio. This made for an intense and trippy atmosphere to create in.

It's one thing spending an hour or two in a club or at a concert with mind and mood-altering lighting effects, and quite another working in such an environment for months on end, and everyone who experienced the *Spirit Of Eden* sessions seems to have had their senses challenged by the situation. It was so dark that musicians had to be led to their performing positions by torchlight, at which point they'd be given headphones on which to listen to the track and then perform what they wanted, with no communication or instruction. The vast majority of performances are said to have been deleted, and those retained for the album were often the less musical notes or even the mistakes.

Perhaps the crowning achievement of the album was the fact that each song was effectively built like a collage made up of many disparate performances (or even singular sounds and tiny musical gestures), creating a piece that sounded like a real, very organic group performing in real-time. In the 21st century, this recording technique is made easy by computer software, but back in 1987/1988, each edit required skill and enormous patience.

Veteran sound engineer Phill Brown – whose career went right back to 1967 and the first Traffic album – was intricately involved in this process, and he would remain on board for *Laughing Stock,* the 'O' Rang project, as well as Mark's solo album. Phill confirms that *Spirit Of Eden* is a collage of literally hundreds of sounds, even though it sounds like a band in a room. 'It sounds like people playing in a room', said Phill, 'but it's all an illusion. Every note is placed there. There are bass tracks that are made up of five different instruments with five or six different players'. Effectively, Mark was sampling live musos. 'Mark would say, "no, this sounds too good, erase it"'.

One example of Mark's detailed and demanding attitude was the time he ordered a semitone alteration to 'Eden', which took Phill and Tim three days of painstaking work with the digital recorder, which was glitching out every few seconds.

Not that there weren't long band jam sessions, of course, which assistant engineer Shaun Lambdin has said 'gave the tracks movement and felt real'. But they were arduous, exhausting sessions, which would usually start mid-morning and generally finish around 2 am the following morning – with a pub break somewhere in the middle.

At some point, Lee and his kit were moved into a hot, sweaty vocal booth, which made him feel divorced from proceedings. The end result, however, was that his drumming on the finished product is superb, and has completely lost the electronically-enhanced patina of his previous work but gained an authoritative, 'organic-machine' feel reminiscent of the great Jaki Leibezeit.

If the demands on Lee were taxing, Paul found that there wasn't much for him to do. Effectively, *Spirit Of Eden* was Mark's project in collaboration with Tim and the aid of Phill, and bandmates Lee and Paul had become session players, and Paul's fretless bass style was needed only sporadically. By the project's end, he was no longer in the band, and would not appear at all on *Laughing Stock.*

Recording was suspended over Christmas 1987 and reconvened on 4 January 1988, specifically for the mixing and vocal overdubs (Mark had taken an earlier break to write lyrics in the country, where his son was born in August). Amazingly, Mark's vocals were recorded quickly, as he'd already honed the lyrics. Not that you can hear what he's singing or even read his scrawled lyrics in the album booklet. It's the sound of Mark's voice that creates meaning in the listener's mind, along with the odd word that crystallizes out of his seemingly intentionally twisted diction.

Everyone involved was burnt out by the intensity of the sessions as well as the length of time it took to make the album. It's somewhat of a relief to learn, however, that the sessions weren't entirely devoid of humour. Phill maintains that a feed was run from the desk to a quarter-inch tape to capture the funny moments between takes, which, if released, could give a whole new angle on things. No one seems to know if these tapes still exist, or whether Mark got to press 'delete' on those as well.

EMI received a cassette of the album on 4 March 1988, and not surprisingly, they were shocked. All that studio time, all that money, and not a single in sight. What happened next was a quagmire of legal crap, with EMI not exercising their option to keep the band until 14 June, a move that Talk Talk declined. 'I knew by this time that EMI was not the company this band should be with', said manager Keith Aspden, 'so I was looking for any way I could get out of the deal'. He argued that Talk Talk were now free because the label had not picked up the option within the contracted three months after 'completion' of the album, and ultimately, the courts would agree.

It was with this testy, unravelling record company relationship hovering in the background that the album was finally released on 12 September 1988. The only concessions Mark had made were to allow an edited version of 'I Believe In You' to be released as a single, and a video clip to be shot (he later claimed that appearing in it made him feel like a prostitute). He also conducted a few interviews, during one of which he made the following pertinent statement about the album: 'It's certainly a reaction to the music that's around at the moment because most of that is shit. It's only radical in the modern context. It's not radical compared to what was happening 20 years ago. If we'd delivered this album to the record company 20 years ago, they wouldn't have batted an eyelid … The important thing was just for it to have the right feel: for it to have an absolute calm, but to have an absolute intensity inside of that'.

There would, of course, be no live dates or TV promo appearances. The initial idea was not to release a single at all. 'We thought we'd broken the mould and turned the tide of history by going back to a world where the single wasn't king', said Tim.

The album title's central idea, said Mark, was two ideas that opposed each other, creation and destruction. 'I've always liked the idea that things that oppose each other can co-exist', he said. Once again, a gorgeous James Marsh painting of various shells and one puffin adorning a tree that appeared to be growing out of the sea was chosen, perhaps suggesting a continuity between *The Colour Of Spring* and *Spirit Of Eden* that wasn't there. (Like most of their covers, the artwork was chosen from Marsh's stash of paintings going back some years. This latest work had been painted in 1975, and was titled 'Fruit Tree').

It was said at the time that EMI hated the album, but it's likely that some staff members liked it and others didn't, and that, moreover, it simply didn't matter whether they were enamoured with it or not. The fact of the matter is that they didn't know how to promote an album with no hits and an unwillingness on the part of the band to participate in getting the word out. Reciprocal animosity between the band, its management, and EMI can't have helped.

On 18 September 1988, *Spirit Of Eden* entered the UK chart at number 19, while the single edit of 'I Believe In You' scraped in at number 85. Both would quickly disappear from the chart, although the album quickly became a critical favourite.

Not long after its release, Mark admitted in an interview that he had no ambition, and that he already had everything he wanted. The next year, on 9 May 1989, Mark's brother Ed, who had been living in squalor, died of gastric poisoning after years of addiction to heroin and other drugs. He was 37. On 23 May 1989, Talk Talk won its case and they were freed from their EMI contract. They would soon announce a deal with Polygram.

'The Rainbow' (Friese-Greene, Hollis)
Twenty-three minutes and 11 seconds. The original CD issue of *Spirit Of Eden* contained only one index point for the first three segued songs, and on the back cover, 'Eden' and 'Desire' were tabulated below and to the right of 'The Rainbow', so I always approached this masterful first half of the album as one song. It turns out that the plan was always to fuse the three songs, but subsequent issues of the album have separated them, so let's look at the three individually.

Mark had expressed his admiration for the German record label ECM, which handpicked superb musicians and recorded them beautifully to create a kind of chamber jazz that was aesthetically as tied to the European classical tradition as it was to improvised jazz. The label's tagline was 'the most beautiful sound next to silence', which ties in perfectly with Mark's perspective on music. 'The Rainbow' starts with a gorgeous suspended orchestral note (mostly strings), just like the ones used in the 1970s by genre-busting ECM artist Eberhard Weber. This hovering note is punctuated by a Wagner-like bowing of bass notes as if to sound a warning. Concurrently, there's the sporadic tootling of a Miles Davis-like trumpet (played by Henry Lowther), and a few eruptions of that dirty-sounding Variophon.

Altogether, this makes for a haunting prelude that fades out by the two-minute mark, at which point the sound spectrum is briefly filled with unidentifiable flying sonic widgets. I've always thought (mistakenly, it turns out) that the spooky, primordial percussion at this point was that of improvising musician Hugh Davies' famous shozygs. (Apparently, the shozyg isn't a specific instrument but consists of fretsaw blades, springs and a ball-bearing mounted inside an encyclopaedia volume. Strange but true!) But while Davies' eccentric contraptions do appear on *Spirit Of Eden,* what we hear on 'The Rainbow' are actually Martin Ditcham's percussion devices, including a rubber mallet scraping along a 'tongue drum' and a metallic baking tray with a triangle striker swirling around.

But there's more! At the 2:16 mark, Tim's debut performance on a dry-sounding electric guitar (apparently a very cheap Vox) rings forth, the riff apparently borrowed from Steppenwolf's 'The Pusher'. That's soon joined by the first of several of the most explosive blues harp (or diatonic harmonica) performances ever taped (Mark Feltham is said to have been made to stand on an 'X' on the studio floor for the best part of a day experimenting with sounds), followed by muted drums and Mark's gently crooning voice.

At what would normally be the chorus (melodically, it is, but there are no repeated stanzas), the beats pause while strings and acoustic piano and church-like organ are added to the mix. Is this pop? Not as we know it! At around the eight-minute mark, the beats cease again and we're back into abstraction, with Davies' whirligigs and Henry Lowther's trumpet adding atmosphere and to provide a link with 'Eden' at 9:05.

The lyric, which references Jimmy Finn from author Mark Twain's *Life On The Mississippi,* seems to be either seeking redemption for the dispossessed or seeking justice for their crimes. I wouldn't hazard a guess and for this fan, it works better as a bunch of indeterminate expressive sounds.

In a podcast, engineer Phill Brown noted that because of the way the individual parts were collaged together, 'it's hard to know whether it's Mark or Tim at any one time playing guitar, or even Robbie McIntosh. Some of the bass parts have five different basses on them!'

Apparently, one of Mark's favourite phrases was: 'What we need is a bit of an explosion'.

Interestingly, at low volume, 'The Rainbow' could almost be played in a café or a church, but turn it up loud and it becomes a monster. And we haven't even started 'Eden' yet.

'Eden' (Friese-Greene, Hollis)

As a whole, *Spirit Of Eden* feels liturgical, and probably the most in-your-face manifestation of this is 'Eden'. 'Everybody needs someone to live by!' sings Mark with all the passion of a preacher at his pulpit, while the organ swells dramatically. In Christian mythology, Eden is the garden in which God first placed man and woman, but despite the religious tone, Mark appears to despair of human limitations. Is he singing about the physical and mental prisons in which we find ourselves, or the need to put your trust in a mere human, who will always ultimately let you down? And is that your romantic partner or some guru? Who knows, but musically and emotionally, every second of its 6:37 is profound and transporting.

Starting with a building beat and strummed guitar, which suddenly breaks out and leads into a quick blast of harmonica and Mark's peerless vocal performance, there's a feeling of great and enduring sorrow mixed with bucolic beauty: emotive, heartbreaking. Mark's voice has become sheer emotion, a human vector of spirituality, or the quest to obtain it.

Precedents? The Van Morrison of *Astral Weeks*, maybe. John Martyn, for sure. Part of the allure of these songs is the tremendous subtlety of their exposition, the way the instruments pull right back to a hushed near silence before suddenly bursting forth with a tremendous noise, with nasty atonal guitar or Feltham's searing harmonica in full overdrive.

Play this song repeatedly and you begin to appreciate the graft that went into its recording, and that part of its peculiar and enduring appeal comes from the fact of it having been assembled from a variety of different sources and even musical moods. When the piece pulls back to a gentle but taut rhythmic canter, with hints of stately piano, then slowly gathers momentum before bursting forth again, the way the instruments are recorded is clearly quite different: the drums and piano sound slightly muffled, with a sense of the room they're recorded in. Feltham's harmonica, on the other hand, sounds like it's piped directly out of an overdriven amp.

I hope Feltham was well paid for these sessions, because it's the incredible sound of his blues harp that sticks in the mind long after you finish listening to *The Spirit Of Eden*. The basis of Feltham's sound is the kind of so-called blues harp played by the likes of Sonny Terry and, in the amplified rock vernacular, J. Geils Band's Magic Dick. Rather than the pleasant chromatic harmonica of the likes of Stevie Wonder, blues harp is capable of really wailing and bending the notes. Feltham takes the instrument to a new level on the Talk Talk sessions, and it's amplified to such an extent that it really bursts out of the speakers. The sound itself is key, because it really feels like the manifestation of the unbelievable pain that the song's narrator is feeling and expressing.

'Desire' (Friese-Greene, Hollis)
Mark is said to have taken the best part of a week to get the guitar sounding the way he wanted it to on 'Desire'. Let's face it: he could probably have wrapped it up in a few hours and achieved a result that his fans would have liked just as much. But it's pointless carping about privilege when the results are undeniably as great as this.

The first notes we hear are from a sorrowful violin, performed in the style of a Norwegian Hardanger fiddle, and promptly joined by a funereal organ and the Variophon. Then a raw guitar riff summons layered trumpets, piano, double bass and dobro. It's like the quiet before a storm and you can feel its menace before all hell breaks loose and finally, rock fans get some release with a few precious bars of incredible noise, drums, guitars — what have you! Then back to the build, and a more extended freak-out, which at last gives Lee a chance to brandish the full power of his drum attack.

In his book (*Are We Still Rolling?*), engineer Phill Brown explains that he was instructed to perform a guitar solo on these sessions (an instrument he can't actually play), and my guess is that the slightly buried guitar squalling on 'Desire' is Phill's.

In the third part of this exquisite trio of songs, Mark's lyrics are once again impossible to interpret definitively, and they're confusing (to say the least). The seeming inference is that desire is overrated: 'That ain't me babe', he sings. 'I'm just content to relax'. Whether he's referring to sexual desire, the desire to achieve, or otherwise, isn't clear.

'Inheritance' (Friese-Greene, Hollis)
At 5:23, the shortest song on the album (and the beginning of Side 2 of the vinyl), on the CD 'Inheritance' begins after an ominous gap of silence

followed by gently tapping cymbals, brushed drums, piano and Danny Thompson's acoustic bass.

It's a discrete piece that takes a bit of getting used to. Less immediate than that first clutch of three songs, it also feels less coherent but grows on repeated hearings. It's not until Mark reaches his emotional vocal peak, along to a burbling organ and horn section, that it comes to life. But then, suddenly, a wind quintet appears, and it feels like we're briefly listening to an experimental modern classical record, before the more familiar elements reappear.

Lyrically, the piece seems to be a meditation on nature's amazing renewal but also a recognition that we're tied to that, regardless of our greedy desire to somehow eclipse our small part in its cycle.

'I Believe In You' (Friese-Greene, Hollis)

Originally titled 'Snow In Berlin' and recorded for *The Colour Of Spring* but not used, 'I Believe In You' was reworked for *Spirit Of Eden*. It would, after all, have been odd to have both 'I Don't Believe In You' and 'I Believe In You' on the same album! And yes, it is a little more accessible than the album's other songs, hence the fact that an edited version was released as the only single. (The band begrudgingly agreed to the single edit but later regretted that decision).

There's another pregnant pause before the detuned guitar sound appears, and then gently tapping drums and piano notes with the sustain pedal down. Mark sings with his customary passion and he almost gulps out the syllables as if the subject was just a little bit too close to the bone.

The 6:11 of 'I Believe In You' is achingly beautiful and drenched in sorrow, the two galvanizing characteristics being the slow groove that allows it to canter along with grace, and the utilisation of an amateur boys' choir towards the end that gives it an almost celestial quality. The song has both trippy and dissonant qualities that make it feel like something of a prequel to the first 'O'Rang album some six years later.

Supposedly referencing brother Ed's heroin addiction, Mark was quoted at the time as saying that it's an anti-heroin song.

'Wealth' (Friese-Greene, Hollis)

Very much an ending song, a quiet but intense way to go out, with just voice, piano and organ. Seemingly a kind of rumination on the value of being bound to love (what's the alternative, after all?), it can't help having an almost hymn-like quality.

Laughing Stock (1991)

Personnel:
Mark Hollis: vocals, guitar, piano, organ, melodica, Variophon
Lee Harris: drums
Tim Friese-Greene: piano, organ, harmonium
Mark Feltham: harmonica
Martin Ditcham: percussion
Robbie McIntosh: guitar, dobro
Levine Andrade, Stephen Tees, George Robertson, Gavyn Wright, Jack Glickman,
Garfield Jackson, Wilf Gibson: viola
Simon Edwards, Ernest Mothle: acoustic bass
Roger Smith, Paul Kegg: cello
Henry Lowther: trumpet, flugelhorn
Dave White: contrabass, clarinet
Produced at Wessex Studios, by Tim Friese-Greene.
Engineered by Phill Brown.
UK release date: 16 September 1991.
Highest chart places: UK: 19
Running time: 41:30

Talk Talk, by now, had already been responsible for two of the finest albums of the 1980s. As improbable as it seems, the group's final album, *Laughing Stock*, would be every bit as great as *Spirit Of Eden*, and possibly even more influential on the hundreds of so-called post-rock bands that rose up in its wake in the 1990s.

Despite rejecting the all-organic, valve-only recording methodology of the previous album, *Laughing Stock* ended up sounding more natural. They had chosen to use a variety of classic microphones (including an old Telefunken U47 valve microphone which was placed 30 feet away from the control room window) and experiment extensively with placement in relation to the instruments. Rather than the close-up recordings of previous albums, Mark's voice and various of the instruments often sound further away, allowing the microphones to pick up the sound of the room itself. Mark didn't want the close-up sound of previous albums, but instead wanted to get the sense of instruments having a physical distance from each other in a space.

Despite this, there are zillions of overdubs and cutting tiny fragments into the compositions (or painting them in), but it *sounds* like a bunch of musicians playing together. Effectively, they used Zappa's xenocrony technique of having musicians solo and then placing fragments of those improvisations into a completely different context.

Legend has it that they spent two days recording a string quartet and kept just one moment – a mistake the cellist had made.

It was a world away from the sparkling sonics of *The Colour Of Spring*, and the sound had an almost lo-fi feel. And where *Spirit Of Eden* – despite its overtly experimental nature – had a smoothness of contour only interrupted by the occasional loud irruption, *Laughing Stock* would have a roughness, a grainy, abrasive edge that was new to Talk Talk.

None of this made it a difficult listening proposition, however. The new emphasis on guitar certainly altered its character, but the album had one ace up its sleeve that brought it into sync with the times.

The early 1990s would see the rise of groups like Massive Attack, whose music would combine sampling and performance with creative studio wizardry and an almost painterly approach to recording, but all with a beat, or groove. Later, Paul and Lee would feed from this scene for their 'O'Rang project. *Laughing Stock* was a world away from Massive Attack, but the majority of its songs would revolve around Lee's drum grooves, which worked their hypnotic way to making the album more easily digestible than it would otherwise have been.

Ironically, despite the album being worked up from the basis of Lee's hard-won beats, by this time, he was no longer a proper member of the group, having been reduced to session muso status, while Paul was gone altogether. This meant that effectively, Talk Talk had become Mark and Tim's project.

There are a couple of factors that might prevent some from savouring its musical wares. Unfortunately, the way *Laughing Stock* was recorded means that it's a middling proposition on a good stereo system. The drums tend to sound like they're coming from another room and, therefore, lack sparkle, and more importantly, dynamic impact. Some music fans like this kind of sound because they somehow evaluate it as being more authentic, but I don't buy that. The meticulous way the album was recorded with literally hundreds of edits hardly screams 'authentic' in the traditional sense. An example of the downside of the album's recording methodology is that the acoustic bass that adorns some of the tracks is compromised, and you simply can't hear its depth or graininess in this 'live' kind of audio environment.

Another downside for some long-term Talk Talk fans is Mark's sheer, unremitting moroseness. There's always been a melancholy aspect to the band, but on *Laughing Stock,* the ebullience of a song like 'Give It Up' is completely absent. If you can handle the fact that on the last two Talk Talk albums, every song is a variation of the same depressive mindset, then it's not a problem. Personally, I can handle *Laughing Stock* in small doses, and can forgive Mark's sometimes oppressive gloominess because it's clear that he also has a pronounced reverence for life, and nature.

So, how did this last Talk Talk album eventuate? Having wriggled out of their contract with EMI, the group was now free to talk turkey with other record companies. Despite *Spirit Of Eden*'s lukewarm commercial response, a bidding war ensued. Paul Munns – who had signed the band to EMI back in 1981 – had moved to Polygram and was keen as mustard. When Mark learned that they could release the album on the Verve imprint, he was in with a grin. Verve, after all, apart from being an important label during the golden age of jazz, had also released the anarchic, genre-busting early albums of Frank Zappa's Mothers Of Invention in the mid-to-late 1960s.

Mark, Tim, Lee and Phill had taken a decent break to recover from the psychic damage caused by the intensity of the *Spirit Of Eden* sessions, so plans were drawn up for their Verve-label debut. The idea was to finish it by late 1989 and release it in early 1990, but nothing would end up going to plan. As it transpired, the album wouldn't be released until 16 September 1991, and the recording sessions would prove so taxing that at its end, the group was effectively finished.

To get things off on the right foot, Mark had bought a flat in London – a bolt-hole to live in away from the family during the album's preparation. Engineer Phill Brown also ended up moving out of his family house and purchasing a flat near to Wessex Studio to be able to fully immerse himself in what transpired to be the intense, year-long recording session.

No fewer than 50 guests/session musicians were invited to participate, but only 18 ended up making the cut after extensive recording (and equally extensive deleting). Mark's idea was to gather like-minded musicians in the studio where 'each player gets to improvise around a basic theme as he or she feels it'. The studio was completely dark apart from oil projections on the walls and ceiling, and a strobe that predictably annoyed the hell out of people.

Unfortunately, the sessions were gruelling, and several participants talk about a very dark, oppressive and uncommunicative atmosphere developing.

Phill wrote in his book: 'I thought the sessions for *Spirit* were intense... until we got into this one. The whole thing was incredibly disorienting'. It was 'psychedelic in the true sense of the word. You'd get to the studio and within an hour be totally unable to remember what time it was or how long you'd been there'. By the end, 'marriages were collapsing, there were breakdowns, people resigning'. He was disappointed in the lack of communication from Mark: 'Most of the time he just stared at his shoes as we three worked'.

They slaved away on a song called 'Swabi' for weeks, but for unknown reasons, Mark couldn't get what he wanted from Lee, who was pushed beyond breaking point, and consequently developed stress-related flu. When he returned from his sickbed, Lee had to perform 24 takes of the song in one day. It is claimed that they wouldn't let Lee hear recordings of his progress. Ultimately, the song was abandoned.

Some songs came together relatively easily. 'Ascension Day' took less than a week, and a planned single version of 'After The Flood' that was shorter and faster was recorded. It was mostly slow going, but by the end of November, six backing tracks had been completed.

'For seven months, we only left the studio to sleep', said Mark in a rare interview. 'Nothing else existed except for the recording, the studio and the nucleus of me, Friese-Green, Phill and Lee Harris'.

With a break for Christmas, they returned in January 1991 to add contributions from guests like Mark Feltham, Martin Ditcham, Henry Lowther and acoustic bassist Simon Edwards, and then in February, they started recording the vocals. Then came the last five-month ordeal: editing the recordings.

'A dark, sarcastic humour permeated these sessions', wrote Phill. 'I remember thinking 'this is the end'', said Tim. 'This is as far as we can go. This will be the last album we make'.

As an outsider, it's hard to understand why Tim, Lee and Phill were so dedicated to achieving Mark's desired accomplishment. Was it a cult mindset that kept them in his spell?

In a podcast, Phill said: 'Mark never got physical, but his verbal humour... it was very intense and damaging to certain people at certain times. Paul left after *Spirit Of Eden* because he got put through the mill. I don't think he felt that he got treated so well, so he went, 'okay, I'm out of this'. Lee hung in there and was paid as a kind of session guy to do *Laughing Stock*. It almost destroyed the guy, it had such a damaging effect and it's hard to explain this because it was all based around what was once humour ... it was this rather non-communication, which Mark was really good at, and the odd comment like 'you really are a cunt'. Lee put up with this, we all did, in a way. It was tough doing *Laughing Stock*. *Spirit Of Eden* was, in a way, quite joyous. There were dark moments, but on the whole, it was such an adventure, because none of us had worked that way before'.

Afterwards, they just walked away from the project, the band, and each other.

Mark disappeared from the music scene for seven years and is said to have decided to be a 'present' father to his two sons.

Polygram's reaction to the tapes when they finally heard them was one of complete incomprehension. David Munns was said to be distraught, and his opinion was that the group hadn't delivered anything 'marketable'. It seems odd that Munns didn't have any prior insight on what he was in for when he signed the band (for a second time). Hadn't he heard *Spirit Of Eden*? Did he expect the group to return to the sound of *The Colour Of Spring*? Surely not. But on this occasion, even Talk Talk's long-time manager, Keith Aspden, was disappointed that Mark hadn't written a 'proper' single; something, anything to help recoup the sizeable advance.

It can't have helped that Mark refused to do anything to promote the album apart from a couple of print media interviews and a Q&A interview tape made by the record company, *Mark Hollis Talks About Laughing Stock,* or that during lunch with the Polydor publicity people he rudely kept his taxi idling outside, promptly leaving without even bidding adieu.

In one of the few interviews of substance, Mark urged fans to fully soak up its magnificence by taking the time to sit and listen while doing nothing else. *Laughing Stock* is packed with Old Testament imagery, with 'Ascension Day', 'After The Flood' and 'Taphead' all apparently referring to dying in sin and being reborn. And on 'New Grass', he sings, 'Someday Christendom may come'. But in the interview, Mark said that he's humanist rather than overtly religious, although he has also been quoted as saying that religion is a good thing and that it's about love.

Laughing Stock was released on 16 September 1991 and hit number 26 on the UK charts before promptly disappearing from view. Ironically, it exited the charts the same week that Nirvana's *Nevermind* shot onto the charts, ushering in a new movement, grunge, that would dominate the rock world for the next few years.

Critical reaction to *Laughing Stock* was gushing, but couldn't save it from imminent oblivion. Mark was compared with genius eccentrics like Brian Wilson, Peter Green and Van Morrison. 'Hollis still works with his characteristic alliteration and assonance, but his lyrics and vocal melodies are no longer fluid, no longer sentences; they're fractured, isolated bursts', wrote one highly impressed reviewer.

As journalist David Stubbs later commented: 'It's renegade albums like this, slipping through the commercial nets, which end up making the whole sordid music business worthwhile'. But perhaps it's the commentary of singer-songwriter Tim Bowness (whose own work reflects a heavy Talk Talk influence) that summed it up best: 'There was an ongoing process of reduction in their music that reminded me of how Samuel Beckett continued to pare down his language in his later work', he wrote in *The Spirit of Talk Talk*. 'Their later albums made most everything else around them seem so artificial that it was sometimes difficult to listen to anything else without being irritated by over-production or stylistic affectations'.

They couldn't have known it at the time, but in effect, Mark and Tim's methodology – of recording musicians independently doing their thing without their knowing the exact context and then placing the performances (or extracts thereof) wherever they saw fit – anticipated the creative sampling boom. As sampling technology became more sophisticated, dilettante DJs and electronic musicians/composers could grab a small musical fragment from someone else's existing song, process it to suit their needs, and insert it into their own work. This technique was used in a cavalier way by hip-hop producers, but the best electronic musicians turned it into an art. I can't help wondering if Mark had been born a decade or two later, would he have taken that path rather than the painful, rigorous and expensive path he chose in the recording of *Spirit Of Eden* and *Laughing Stock*?

Laughing Stock would go on to be named by *Pitchfork* as the 11th best album of the 1990s, while *Stylus* magazine named it the greatest post-rock album. Meanwhile, Polygram quietly deleted this masterwork from their catalogue just a few months after its release. (It was reissued in 2006 by its parent group Universal).

'Myrrhman' (Hollis, Friese-Greene)

Reviewer Ian Cranna made the point that *Laughing Stock* 'is divided into six parts although it's really one long piece spanning an evolution of moods', and he's right. Like *Spirit Of Eden,* each track feels like it shares most of its musical DNA with all the others, but not in an obvious way like the variations of a theme on a 1970s progressive rock album.

If you've got the volume low, you'll think that the album begins with silence, but in fact, the first 15 seconds are made up of amplifier hiss.

At first, the album can sound quite brittle compared to *Spirit Of Eden* as there's more 'live' ambience and overtones/feedback/hum. But the more you listen, it mellows out and you adjust your senses. It's the emotional weight that bends you out of shape as the picture starts to coalesce and make sense.

Eventually, the reverbed guitar is sounded. Mark's voice is the focus and it's a gentle and anguished instrument, but behind it is a horn-laced sound that's imbued with deep melancholy, like Miles Davis at a funeral. There's a little double bass, a touch of piano, a flourish or two of drums, but it's all muted, disconsolate. Then some even more devastatingly sad-sounding strings and wind instruments are added. It makes you want to weep. Can it get more intense? Finally, there's a dusty-sounding violin. Is this rock? Not really. It's a eulogy, but what to?

Well, some have suggested that this may be a song about suicide; that myrrh is a gum resin that was used to embalm mummies in ancient Egypt, and that Mark's lyrics about placing a chair at the backroom door, 'Help me up/I can't wait anymore' are about hanging yourself. But given that Mark survived some 27 years after this before cancer finally felled him suggests otherwise.

Regardless, it's an exceptionally gloomy, doom-laden way to start an album, and feels more like an epilogue.

'Ascension Day' (Hollis, Friese-Greene)

This is 'pop music' by comparison, or at least, that seems to be the case at the start. Lee's drums set up a beat that sounds alarmingly close to those of the machine-like repetitions of Kraut rock legend, Jaki Liebezeit (Can). There's also double bass and a sinuous, rather gorgeous, repeated hollow-bodied guitar figure, deliciously sounding over and over again.

But soon, however, a second guitar enters with a furious, intense one-chord blast of shrapnel-laden noise, before Mark's vocal finally asserts itself.

This song must have inspired the whole quiet/loud post-rock contingent, as it has some deliciously detailed soft sections, contrasted by the incredible intensity of that angry guitar.

Rather than the supernatural apparition it felt like on the two previous albums, Feltham's harmonica is on an equal footing, volume-wise, to the other instruments, bringing the fine Long Beach group War to mind, and, specifically, their harmonica player, Lee Oskar.

It gets to the point where Tim or Mark (presumably the latter) just keeps slamming the one chord on guitar, getting more and more intense, until it's brutally cut off at the end, leaving you in shock and your ears ringing.

Seemingly about the job of redeeming one's sins for judgement day and the possibility of ascending to heaven, 'Ascension Day' was the album's third single, released in November 1991.

'After The Flood' (Hollis, Friese-Greene)

Engineer Phill Brown is on record (ha-ha) as saying that 'After The Flood' represents 'probably the best engineering for me in the past 40 years'. Phill is an old-school engineer who began his career in 1967 and has worked for everyone from Jimi Hendrix to Robert Palmer, so it's not surprising that he prefers recording 'au natural' where the sounds have the feel of a real performance in a real space.

It's certainly an intoxicating track, but to my ears on a high-end audio system, it lacks definition and, while it begs to be played loud, the sound is ultimately banded together in the mid-range. It probably sounded a whole lot better in the studio, but Polydor/Universal has never seen fit to issue a properly remastered version of *Laughing Stock*. While there was a belated vinyl issue in 2016, it felt even less dynamic than the CD version and many customers complained of clicks and pops.

The second-to-longest track at 9:39, 'After The Flood' appears to be another of Mark's references to the Biblical story of Noah's Ark and the so-called 'great flood', an event brought on by Cain murdering his brother, Abel.

The piece gets underway with a dreamy piano and a cute-sounding, slightly haunting Variophon. Harmonica gently wails as the drums slowly get louder, playing those same heavy-hitting Kraut-like patterns. Then a change to major key and church organ brings in a sanctimonious atmosphere for just a moment before Mark sings the first verse.

The sound of Lee's drums together with the deep bass is once again like a preview of where Lee and Paul would soon head with 'O'Rang.

Mark's vocal gets more demonstrative but then pulls back for a reflective moment or two, at which point a gaggle of geese in distress appear – in reality, it's a Variophon being mishandled! It's an extraordinarily uncomfortable sound that seems to go on for much longer than it does, at which point the church-like organ returns to offer some solace, and Mark returns with another few verses and a vocal that's both reflective and agitated in turns.

Finally, the original Variophon figure returns while the drums continue their relentless, monotonous path and fade away.

A different, edited version of this song was released as the first single from the album in September 1991.

'Taphead' (Hollis, Friese-Greene)

Interestingly, on the UK CD pressing, the solo guitar figure that's so integral to 'Taphead' intrudes on the last seconds of 'After The Flood' and the two pieces segue. On the American CD pressing, there's silence between the tracks and several seconds of atonal guitar that's not on the UK CD.

The guitar figure that opens it (on the lower notes) is reminiscent of Rain Tree Crow's 'Any Colour You Are', from the reformation project of Japan members that came out in March 1991. Could Mark or Tim have heard that song and subconsciously absorbed its riff, or is it simply coincidence?

The already spare guitar figure devolves as Mark sings in a tremulous, vastly unhappy voice that you either find brilliant or makes you want to slap him and say, 'cheer up!'

The sound field slowly fills with a hellish background concatenation of horn and woodwind instruments, over which blows an ear-splitting fanfare of trumpets. There's just a hint of blues harp between the trumpet blasts. It's a scary deluge of dissonant ambience with an undertow of orchestral depression.

Not an easy listen, 'Taphead' overall is probably the most difficult track on *Laughing Stock*, as it feels very much like Mark is falling to pieces, an emotional mess. It finally fades out during a hovering organ note.

'New Grass' (Hollis, Friese-Greene)
It took 11 long days to mix the 9:47 running time of 'New Grass'. Later, Elbow's Guy Garvey would proclaim it the most beautiful song he'd ever heard, and many Talk Talk fans appear to agree.

Once again, Lee's splendid tap-tap-tap-bonk drumming boils away and Mark's hollow-bodied guitar sound is resplendent in clusters. An organ bubbles with conviction, and finally, Mark's vocal is so intense and almost 'gone' that it's like he's saying goodbye.

There are liturgical piano notes and chording, a folkish violin drone, and again, lengthy sections with no vocals at all.

Mark's vocal isn't especially high in the mix, as though he wants it to be on an equal footing with the other instruments. It's like he wants his voice to be pure expression. It's also like he's preparing to disappear.

With its line 'Someday Christendom may come', it's tempting to read religious inferences into 'New Grass', but it could equally be about simply finding peace, or redemption, or transcending redemption and accepting pure spirituality.

A cynic might feel emboldened to claim that it's a song where nothing much happens. It's true that the listener needs to cultivate the right mindset to appreciate that what might seem excessively repetitious is in fact, that way for a purpose. In fact, its minimalism allows many small variations and events to stand out in a way that would otherwise be impossible.

Still, it's hard to imagine why anyone would release 'New Grass' as a single. It was the second single from the album, released on 28 October 1991.

'Runeii' (Hollis, Friese-Greene)
For all intents and purposes, *Laughing Stock* ends with 'New Grass'. 'Runeii' is so minimal and desolate that it's more like an epilogue.

It begins with a lone and lonesome guitar, resonating like an Indian sitar, complete with hum and extraneous noise. Mark sounds disconsolate and almost past caring, inevitably more self-aware but equally as bereft-sounding as Nick Drake on his last recordings. The organ sings sweetly and the gnarly guitar plays quietly, Mark's voice almost mirroring the guitar notes.

There are no drums on the last-ever Talk Talk song, just piano way down in the mix. And then it finishes to just the hum, and unceremoniously cuts off.

What a way to end the album, and the artistic life, of Talk Talk, with a song that seems past caring, as though the worst has already happened but sending out the vibe that happiness is very definitely not easy.

The Compilations

There's no denying that with a group like Talk Talk, the studio albums are pretty much all you need. They're what the group intended, in the running order the band devised. Greatest hits compilations have a place, especially when a group has a long list of successful singles and we want to hear them all together. But in Talk Talk's case, while there were a few earworm singles on each of the first three albums, all that was over for their last two.

In Talk Talk's case, a compilation is only really justified when the singles are substantially different to the album versions, or the songs themselves are alternative or demo takes, or never-before-released.

As we shall see, EMI has mercilessly milked the group's catalogue to a degree that you can't help but wonder whether it was sometimes out of spite. It's clear that EMI was unhappy with *Spirit Of Eden* and not surprising that they sought to claw back some of the cash they will have seen as wasted on a non-commercial product. However, their cavalier and disrespectful attitude to the group and its remarkable catalogue ends up debasing and diluting their music.

Nevertheless, there are a couple of Talk Talk compilations of some merit, for reasons I'll explain below.

I don't see the point in rambling on about releases that don't justify their existence except as financial exploitation, so excuse me if the majority of these compilation descriptions are brief.

It's My Mix (1985)
This 1985 album was released in only two markets: Italy and Canada. It's notable for being the first album of collected remix 12" singles, and not much else.

'Why Is It So Hard?' (12" US Remix)
'Talk Talk' (12" US Remix)
'My Foolish Friend (12" Mix)
'It's My Life' (12" Mix)
'Dum Dum Girl' (12" Mix)
'Such A Shame' (12" US Remix)

Mini-LP (1986)
As with *It's My Mix*, Talk Talk's *Mini LP* is notable for being released in 1986, some years before the first 'proper' Talk Talk album of remixes, but it was available in Greece only.

'Such A Shame' (US 12" Mix)
'Living In Another World' (US 12" Mix)
'Life's What You Make It' (Extended Version)
'It's My Life' (Extended Version)
'Talk Talk' (Extended Version)

Above: Talk Talk quickly became averse to endless promo 'opportunities' and photo sessions. In this off-the-cuff 1985 shot, they look unusually relaxed. From left to right: Lee Harris, Mark Hollis and Paul Webb. (*Rose Christian*)

Left: The first Talk Talk album (1982) and the beginning of a career-long association with artist James Marsh. Neither the artist nor the group had quite found its niche. (*Universal*)

Right: Released in April 1982, 'Talk Talk' was the second single from the debut album and far from a hit at the time, despite its intrinsic catchiness. (*Universal*)

Left: Released in February 1984, *It's My Life* was a vast improvement over the group's debut and marked the beginning of Tim Friese-Greene's involvement. (*Universal*)

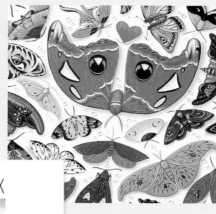

TALK TALK · THE COLOUR OF SPRING

Right: Everything came together beautifully for the group's third album, *The Colour Of Spring* (1986), a smash success featuring their best-known hits. (*Universal*)

TALK TALK

SPIRIT OF EDEN

Left: Despite its iconic James Marsh artwork, *Spirit Of Eden* was a step too far for many pop fans, but it changed the face of contemporary music. (*Universal*)

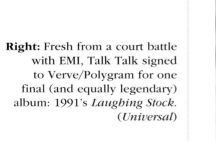

TALK TALK

LAUGHING STOCK

Right: Fresh from a court battle with EMI, Talk Talk signed to Verve/Polygram for one final (and equally legendary) album: 1991's *Laughing Stock*. (*Universal*)

Above: Manufactured by EMI in the hope that Talk Talk would prove as monetarily successful as Duran Duran, this white garb look was ditched by the group as soon as the opportunity presented itself!

Below: A touring version of the group lining up in Germany in 1984. From left to right: John Hook (guitar), Lee Harris (drums), Mark Hollis (voice), Paul Webb (bass), Ian Curnow (keys). (*Alamy*)

Above: Having well and truly thrown off their new romantic garb, Talk Talk look themselves in 1986: Paul Webb, Mark Hollis, Lee Harris. (*dpa Picture Alliance*)

Below: Note Mark Hollis's ever-present shades, worn inside and out as an effective defence mechanism. (*Rob Verhorst*)

Above: A rare pic of Mark's late 1970s pre-Talk Talk group, The Reaction. (*Mark Jordan*)

Below: This is the classic image of Mark issuing forth with pitch-perfect renditions of classic songs during 1986, in this case, Montreux. (*Gérald Bosshard*)

Above: Mark letting his hair down and out on the last-ever TT tour to promote *The Colour Of Spring* in 1986. (*Alamy*)

Below: The touring band appearing on Italian TV in 1986. Clockwise: Phil Ramocon, Lee Harris, Ian Curnow, Mark Hollis, Paul Webb. (*Alamy*)

Left: The music video for 'Talk Talk' sees the group in its infancy playing the record company game. (*Universal*)

Right: In the music video for 'It's My Life', Mark appears in a zoo, intentionally not mouthing the lines.

Left: Another shot from the 'zoo' video clip for 'It's My Life'.

Right and below: In this innovative-for-its-time music video for 'Life's What You Make It', the group 'perform' outside at night amongst creatures and creepy crawlies.

Right: A spectral-looking Hollis in the reflective music video for *Spirit Of Eden*'s 'I Believe In You'.

Left: Tim Friese-Greene during the legendary *Spirit Of Eden* sessions playing Hammond organ in the dark at Wessex Studio, with a strobe inside a clear bucket! (*Phill Brown*)

Right: Master tapes in the bag! *Spirit Of Eden* done and dusted. The various 48 reels of 2-inch tape are displayed here. (*Phill Brown*)

Left: The brilliant Focusrite desk used in the making of the self-titled Mark Hollis solo album. The desk had 80 channels, but only two of them were used! (*Phill Brown*)

This page: Despite typically shying away from publicity, Mark Hollis happily chats with fans at a *Spirit Of Eden* signing session in the Netherlands on 18 August 1988. Talk Talk fan Albert Voorhorst won a competition to meet the band. Only Mark from the band was there, but Albert says: 'He talked to us for something like an hour' and that he was in no hurry to get back to his hotel. (*Albert Voorhorst*)

Mark Hollis

Left: The Mark Hollis solo album – originally planned as a Talk Talk album – was released to little fanfare or publicity in January 1998 and never troubled the charts. (*Universal*)

Right: Paul Webb and Lee Harris formed 'O' Rang after Talk Talk and released this incredibly heady, psychedelic and guest-studded fusion album in 1994. (*Echo*)

.O.RANG
FIELDS AND WAVES

'O'RANG

Herd Of Instinct

Left: 'O' Rang's second and final album, *Fields And Waves* (1996) was a much more pared-down project that led the way towards Paul's Rustin Man project. (*Echo*)

Right: Paul's first album under the Rustin Man nom de plume was this 2002 collaboration with Portishead's Beth Gibbons. (*Universal*)

Left: Rustin Man's solo debut *Drift Code* was released in February 2019 and displayed Paul's prowess as a singer-songwriter. (*Domino*)

Right: *Clockdust* was the follow-up to *Drift Code* and – recorded concurrently over many years – featured contributions from Lee Harris.

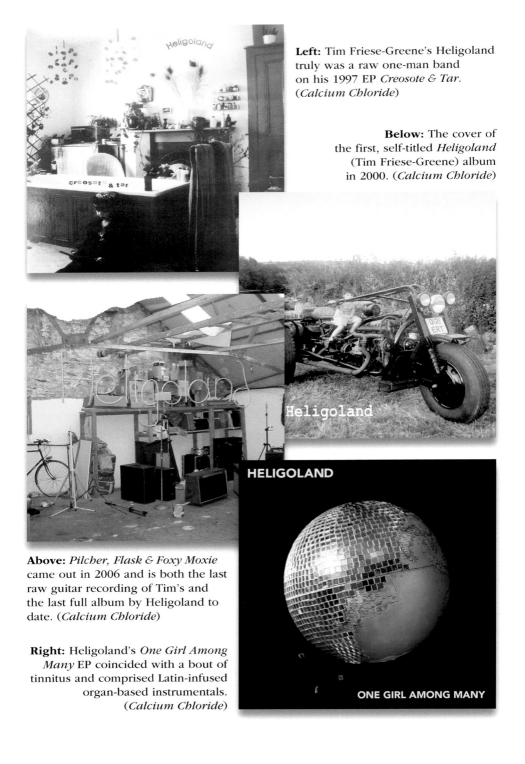

Left: Tim Friese-Greene's Heligoland truly was a raw one-man band on his 1997 EP *Creosote & Tar*. (*Calcium Chloride*)

Below: The cover of the first, self-titled *Heligoland* (Tim Friese-Greene) album in 2000. (*Calcium Chloride*)

Above: *Pilcher, Flask & Foxy Moxie* came out in 2006 and is both the last raw guitar recording of Tim's and the last full album by Heligoland to date. (*Calcium Chloride*)

Right: Heligoland's *One Girl Among Many* EP coincided with a bout of tinnitus and comprised Latin-infused organ-based instrumentals. (*Calcium Chloride*)

ONE GIRL AMONG MANY

Right: Tim's *10 Sketches For Piano Trio* was an odd 'virtual jazz' album. (*Calcium Chloride*)

Below: Recorded during the Covid meltdown in 2020, *Melodic Apoptosis* is a bizarre easy listening, 'exotica'-influenced record. (*Calcium Chloride*)

TIM FRIESE-GREENE

10 SKETCHES FOR PIANO TRIO

TIM FRIESE-GREENE
MELODIC APOPTOSIS

SHORT-HAIRED DOMESTIC

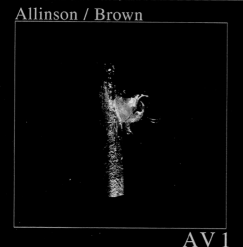

Allinson / Brown

AV 1

Above: *Short-haired Domestic* is Tim's first collaboration with his partner Lee, who sings each of its songs in a different language! (*Calcium Chloride*)

Left: Originally an art installation, the moody Allinson/Brown project exploits the skills of Talk Talk engineer Phill Brown and features guest artist Mark Hollis. (*Resurgence*)

Above: A poptastic shot of Talk Talk from a Dutch teen publication. (*Albert Voorhorst*)

Right: A shot of a smiling Mark Hollis taken in 1990, the year before the final Talk Talk album *Laughing Stock*. (*Martyn Goodacre*)

Natural History: The Very Best Of Talk Talk (1990)

If all you wanted of Talk Talk was the hits and more well-known numbers from the first three albums, then *Natural History: The Very Best Of Talk Talk* would have done very nicely. Released in June 1990, it might have remained in your Sony Discman for months.

Talk Talk at the time were philosophical about this unauthorised release. Clearly, EMI were pissed off with them and keen to recoup some of the losses on *Spirit Of Eden*. Mark wasn't happy with it, however, as it represented a version of Talk Talk that no longer existed and which he'd long moved on from, and here it was, rapidly becoming the most successful Talk Talk album ever, reaching number four on the charts and selling more than a million copies.

A chronological sampling, the album took two songs from *The Party's Over*, three from *It's My Life*, and a whopping four songs (half the album!) from *The Colour Of Spring*, followed by the two most accessible songs from *Spirit Of Eden*. It gratuitously added two songs recorded live at the Hammersmith Odeon, which would later appear on the *London 1986* album. A 2007 reissue of *Natural History: The Very Best Of Talk Talk* would somewhat oddly add the 1983 single, 'My Foolish Friend' (Brenner/Hollis), which hadn't previously appeared on an album. While it does its job, by gutting the four albums it mines, it shows a level of disrespect towards the band and their fans.

'**Today**' (Brenner, Harris, Hollis, Webb)
'**Talk Talk**' (Hollis, Hollis)
'**My Foolish Friend**' (Brenner, Hollis)
'**Such A Shame**' (Hollis)
'**Dum Dum Girl**' (Friese-Greene, Hollis)
'**It's My Life**' (Friese-Greene, Hollis)
'**Give It Up**' (Friese-Greene, Hollis)
'**Living In Another World**' (Friese-Greene, Hollis)
'**Life's What You Make It**' (Friese-Greene, Hollis)
'**Happiness Is Easy**' (Friese-Greene, Hollis)
'**I Believe In You**' (Friese-Greene, Hollis)
'**Desire**' (Friese-Greene, Hollis)
'**Life's What You Make It**' (Friese-Greene, Hollis) – Live at the Hammersmith Odeon
'**Tomorrow's Started**' (Friese-Greene, Hollis) – Live at the Hammersmith Odeon

History Revisited: The Remixes (1991)

If Mark, Lee, Paul and Tim thought that the above 'best of' was the worst EMI could throw at them, they were mistaken. For being difficult bastards, they would have to suffer the indignity of having their hard-won and carefully crafted songs defiled by a bunch of DJs on the 1991 release, *History Revisited: The Remixes*.

It beggars belief that EMI would take it upon themselves to commission miscellaneous DJs to mutilate the Talk Talk catalogue for the burgeoning dance music market, without so much as asking permission.

It's not that Talk Talk were above having their work remixed – in fact, as was the trend in the 1980s, 12" singles with extended mixes and dub versions were routinely released by the band, especially in the first few years when their sound was still pop-oriented and shiny. (In fact, *Asides Besides* was a double CD compilation of exactly those mixes.) It was the thing to do in the synth-pop years and a lot of the time, the key aspects of a song retained their integrity.

But not this time. It's not surprising that Mark was furious about *History Revisited: The Remixes*. 'It's outrageous to give my songs like this to people who I wouldn't work with in my worst nightmares', he said. 'They've bastardised my work without my knowledge – they should be ashamed of themselves'.

The album leapt off the shelves, but the remixes were mostly downright embarrassing. EMI had commissioned the mixes from mostly obscure DJs with no connection to the group or feeling for their music. It's a horribly botched affair, with many of the DJs making aesthetically dubious (to say the least) choices.

Another issue is the poor quality of the sonics. The usual exacting near-audiophile standard of engineering and mastering hasn't been applied. In other words, the production lacks sonic depth or dynamics. While the 12" singles the band released during its lifetime sparkle with all of the expected impact – low bass and kick-ass drums, for instance – *History Revisited: The Remixes* sounds dull and completely lacks any sonic sparkle.

At their best, remixes allow the fan to hear a tune from fresh perspective. At their worst, it's just some anonymous DJ ruining a tune. Much of the time here, the latter pertains.

EMI would have to pay for their sins, Talk Talk taking them to court, where the record company was made to delete and destroy the album. But because so many were already in the market, even 30 years later, it's easy to find second-hand copies.

'Living In Another World '91' – Remixed by Julian Mendelsohn

One of the few real-name remixers here, Julian Mendelsohn has done good work producing a variety of bands, including Pet Shop Boys, Level 42, The Associates and even Paul McCartney. True to form, he doesn't fiddle with the formula too much. His only real contribution is a bit more groove and boosted bass. In other words, why bother?

'Such A Shame' – Remixed by Gary Miller

Producer/musician Gary Miller remixes three songs here on *History Revisited: The Remixes* and his are amongst the worst offenders. This is odd in a way because Miller (who died at the age of 62 in May 2022) had a decent track record and even went on to work with the likes of Simply Red and David

Bowie. It should be noted, however, that at this time, he was one of the production team at the much-derided Stock Aitken & Waterman, purveyors of generic commercial crap by the likes of Kylie Minogue, Jason Donovan, Rick Astley and Samantha Fox. It feels almost as if he hates Talk Talk for being too good. The track starts with some kind of wildly inappropriate African chant (like it came off a Deep Forest record, for fuck's sake). There's a big bass groove, sundry other samples, but big chunks of the song are missing. The groove is a light house beat. It doesn't work at all.

'Happiness Is Easy (Dub)' – Remixed by Paul Webb and Lee Harris
This is the one track that's listenable, and the reason is obvious. It's simply a dub mix of the song, something that was common back then: on the A-side would be the current single, maybe an extended version, and on the B-side would be the dub version, Jamaican-style, with various of the layers subtracted and added and generally loads of echo and some experimentation with the mix, and then just a ghostly echo of the singer (and in this case the children's choir as well.) This is big on percussion (drums, conga) and acoustic bass. It does a nice job of isolating elements. Note: A sonically superior version of this is available on *Asides Besides*.

'Today' – Remixed by Gary Miller
The dire Gary Miller again. No idea what the voice samples are, but they don't work, and the generic '80s dance mix just ruins it. Go back to Stock Aitken Waterman, you fool!

'Dum Dum Girl (Spice Remix)' – Remixed by Justin Robertson
Justin Robertson (aka The Prankster) did loads of remixes in the 1980s and 1990s, from Bjork to the Charlatans to The Chemical Brothers to Fatboy Slim. He seems to have been a go-to guy, but here, he can't resist adding silly samples and a big beat dance mix, stripping everything else out except Mark's voice. Truly horrid.

'Life's What You Make It' – Remixed by BBG
Remixer BBG seems to have fallen into obscurity, and I'm not surprised. It's just so dull. He uses jungle sounds and the mix is very electronic. Hardly any of the song is evident for the first minute, and then finally, the piano line, and Mark. Otherwise, it has an inappropriately galloping electronic beat and a bit of synth. The guitar and vocal is utilised at times, but way back in the mix.

'Talk Talk' – Remixed by Gary Miller
Miller must have given EMI a fee reduction for the three mixed tracks. It's hard to think of another reason for his inclusion at all. This generic jazzy house groove goes on and on, and on!

'It's My Life' (Tropical Rainforest Mix) – Remixed by Dominic Woosey and JJ Montana
This took *two* people to remix it! Woosey appears to have been quite a prolific trance producer, while JJ Montana is a DJ of sorts. This is possibly the worst track, with a water feature, plinky-plonk rhythm, bongos, monkeys and even sheep! WTF are *sheep* doing in a tropical rainforest? No wonder Mark was incensed by this nonsense!

'Living In Another World (Curious Dub Mix)' – Remixed by 4 To The Floor
Four to the floor is such a generic descriptor of house-based dance music that who knows (or cares) who these remixers are, anyway? It boasts a solid beat, a deeper bass, and is essentially, as it says, a dub instrumental. But as with several other tracks, the samples used are inappropriate and embarrassing.

'Life's What You Make It (The Fluke Remix)' – Remixed by Fluke
Fluke was an electronic band from the late '80s with several of their own records. Later, they went into gaming and soundtrack work. This makes the famous chords sound like an electro-pop ditty. But overall, it's one of the better cuts because it meddles with the song less.

The Very Best Of Talk Talk (1997)
Not to be confused with *Natural History: The Very Best Of Talk Talk* (1990), this 1997 compilation, includes the single versions of 'Today' and 'I Believe In You', as well as the Rhett Davies re-recording of 'Talk Talk' and the original version of 'Such A Shame'. A fair rather than definitive compile, it was released to coincide with the individual remastered albums and the gathering-together of otherwise unavailable odds and sods that was *Asides Besides*.

'It's My Life'
'Talk Talk' (single version)
'Today' (single version)
'Dum Dum Girl
'Have You Heard The News?'
'Such A Shame' (original version)
'For What It's Worth'
'Life's What You Make It'
'Eden' (edit)
'April 5th**'**
'Living In Another World' (single version)
'I Believe In You' (single version)
'Give It Up' (single version)

'John Cope'
'Wealth'
'Time It's Time'

Asides Besides (1997)

While EMI mercilessly exploited the Talk Talk back catalogue, they also saw that each of their albums was lovingly remastered in 1997 and put together *Asides Besides*, a double CD that's essential for any dedicated fan.

It might seem odd pairing an album of the 12" mixes they did for their first three albums with an album of offcuts and rarities, but the two discs make a useful contrast. And for those who only wanted the extended mixes, this disc was to be issued again by itself the following year under the title *12x12 Original Remixes*, and yet again in 2001 as simply *Remixed*.

It's worth reiterating that the 12 versions on Disc 1 expose *History Revisited: The Remixes* for the bogus product it was. Talk Talk fans who are just interested in the original songs won't see the value in these extended versions, some of which are proper remixes and others of which are dub oriented. But those of us who experienced the early-to-mid-'80s phenomenon of the 12" extended mix single will have relished the chance to revisit these discs without having to haul the original vinyl out of storage.

It's also worth reflecting on the era and how much fun it was. It wasn't just the most crassly commercial groups releasing extended 12" singles in the '80s. Even bands like The Cure, Echo & The Bunnymen and Siouxsie & The Banshees utilised the medium. It gave the bands and their producers/engineers a chance to go a bit hog-wild with sonics and beef up the bass, given that a 12" single enabled deeper grooves and better tracking of a stylus. And after some years of gloomy, monochrome post-punk and new-wave presentations, suddenly, it wasn't a crime to dance.

Suffice to say that 12" singles were all the rage during the new romantic era in which the group existed, and it became obligatory for bands to release extended mixes, sometimes just for the 'extra bandwidth' (fatter sound) that was available via 12". Sometimes the songs were exactly the same as the 7" versions, but more often groups took advantage of the extra space to juice things up, add some fat bass or use 'dub' effects to cut a track that was more club friendly. This is the case with the 12 songs on this CD.

Annoyingly, there's scant remix information on the package about individual songs, but at least we know that these were all sanctioned by the band, and their sonic fidelity is really great.

Disc 1

'Talk Talk' (Extended Version)

It's worth noting that at 4:35, 'Talk Talk' isn't much longer than the album cut at 3:23. They stick a few bars of silly synth nonsense in and some club-footed beats, then Mark's voice is echoed and processed. There's a Burundi-style drum break and enhanced cowbells. It's quite sonically impactful but needs to be longer. There's no information as to who did the mix, so presumably, it was producer Colin Thurston.

'Today' (Extended Version)

Again, at only 4:34, it's hardly extended, and certainly fails to take advantage of the extra length availed by the 12-inch format, but despite this, it's a bit radical. Mike Robinson (engineer/mixer on *The Party's Over*) adds snapping percussion echoing across the stereo field and drum machine claps. Mark's voice is lengthened on 'Today it's a dream awaaaaaay!' Then, there's an electronic drum orgy with repeated vocal snippets and odd noises before cutting back to the song. It's hard to imagine Mark being happy with the way the song is meddled with here, but it's quite entertaining, nevertheless.

'My Foolish Friend' (Extended Version)

Once again, there's only a producer credit (Rhett Davies). This mix shows a different, more electronic slant to the group, had Mark wanted to explore that. (But we all know what he thought of synthetic instruments). The drums crackle like a recurrent horsewhip and the bass is big and lumpy. The song is too slow and maudlin to want to dance to, however.

'It's My Life' (Extended Version)

Remixed by Tim Friese-Greene, at 6:19, 'It's My Life' has room for some jungle birds, and some big bass and drum stuff. The puff/exhalation of the synth is emphasized, as is the strummed acoustic guitar and fulsome jingle bells. The breakdown is drum-heavy, with echoed voice and synth.

'Such A Shame' (Extended Version)

Again remixed by Tim, at 7:01, there's room to breathe and time for some drum and synthesizer stuff before we get to the song proper. It sounds very crisp and deep. Mark's voice is echoed: 'It's a shame-ame-ame...' Paul's New Order-like bass is heightened (or should we say deepened) on a mix that keeps most of the core song together but also breaks out in sonically adventurous ways. There's a section with almost industrial drums and scary sound effects. Enjoyable!

'Dum Dum Girl' (12" Mix)

Remixed by Steve Thompson, an American producer who has worked with everyone from Madonna to Korn, this version of 'Dum Dum Girl' keeps most of the core ingredients and simply goes for bigger and bolder, with everything sounding as clear as a bell. There's a brief section where it changes tempo for a few bars and goes a bit manic. The guitar solo is given extra resonance.

'Without You' (12" Mix)

Produced (rather than remixed) by Tim, this 'Dum Dum Girl' B-side is a bit dull and at 5:54, without any obvious concessions to the 12" format, feels overlong.

'Life's What You Make It' (Extended Mix)

Occasionally, an album version is already such a spectacular mix that it's simply impossible to better. Such is the case for this classic from *The Colour Of Spring*. Remixed by Tim, it feels like it's been slowed down to a crawl, although that observation may be merely perceptual. The bass is beefed up, which eliminates some of the textural finesse, but whiffs of electric guitar here and synth there do their best to justify its 12" existence.

'Living In Another World' (Extended Remix)

The longest cut on the whole album at 8:58, it's remixed by Gavin MacKillop, a well-known engineer who has worked with (amongst many others) Echo & The Bunnymen, Shriekback and Public Image. With bongos and big drums and stereo percussion, it's bigger, louder, but ultimately less cohesive than many of the other mixes. Again, it's hard to better (or even provide a different slant to) the album version.

'Pictures Of Bernadette' (Dance Mix)

Once again, Tim is credited as producer, but not remixer. Another long one at 8:06, it's hard to see the point of this as it doesn't make you want to dance, and is more of an oddity than anything. The drums and percussion are again effectively prominent on a track that at one point feels like it wants to turn into a blue-eyed '60s soul revue but then thinks better of it.

'Happiness Is Easy' (12" Mix)

Remixed by Paul and Lee, the acoustic bass is cranked right up, which is thrilling but necessarily means that it loses its textural grace. There are bongos, and the piano and keyboards sound more dreamy and semi-ambient than the album version. There are simply echoed fragments of Mark's vocal along with sliced and diced segments of the children's choir. Don't go buying *History Revisited: The Mixes* for this track, as it's mastered so much more deeply and clearly here.

'Such A Shame' (Dub Mix)

Steve Thompson is back again on the mix. There's a lot of echoed, chattering drums and percussion, along with sounds being distended and distorted and otherwise put under the microscope. Nice enough.

Disc 2:

Useful for Talk Talk fans who already have everything else, this second disc of *Asides Besides* is really for those who feel that they need demo versions

of songs they already know as well as B-sides of singles, and single edits/
versions. By no means a 'must-have'; it's for those who simply can't get
enough.

'Talk Talk' (Demo)
'Mirror Man' (Demo)
'Candy' (Demo)

'Talk Talk', 'Mirror Man' and 'Candy' appear here in slightly rough (but far
from ragged) demo form. If you were enough of a Talk Talk fan that you
picked up the limited double 7" single of 'Such A Shame' – all of which
featured as part of that package – then you already have them. Mark's vocals
sound really amped up, but the synth playing (especially on 'Mirror Man')
needs some refinement. The later versions are much better, but these have
a certain new-wave charm without the somewhat compromising production
gloss of *The Party's Over*.

'Strike Up The Band'

The B-side of 'Mirror Man', this is about as dated as any early '80s track could
be. There are elements that could fit happily into later Hollis pieces, but the
style is horribly hokey.

'?'

The song with just a question mark as a title, '?' is another song that's
hopelessly landlocked to a time and place, but worth hearing against the
group's better compositions/performances. Like 'Strike Up The Band' it sounds
more like early Ultravox or even NZ/Australian synth-rock group Mi-sex.

'My Foolish Friend'

Unlike the other tracks, the 1983 non-album single, 'My Foolish Friend', had
already appeared on the 1990 best-of, *Natural History*. One of their best early
songs, with a typically impassioned vocal and a memorable chorus; it's hard
to figure out why it didn't make it to an album at the time.

'Call In The Night Boy' (Piano Version)

An acoustic version of the B-side of 'My Foolish Friend', this song is worth the
price of admission alone. Beginning with a bracing piano flurry, and then some
curly bass and stately cello, Mark's vocal is indicative of where he was heading.
This song, together with 'For What It's Worth', 'It's Getting Late In The Evening'
and 'John Cope', also appeared on 2003's *Introducing... Talk Talk* compilation.

'Why Is It So Hard?'

This obscure song appears to have only been released back in 1985 in Italy,
but amazingly, there are several different unreleased versions floating about
amongst fan groups.

'Again A Game... Again'

This B-side of 'Such A Shame' fits right into that era of the group. Slick and shiny, with a particularly emotive performance by Mark and loads of synth. This would have been strong enough for inclusion on an album.

'Without You'

The B-side of 'Dum Dum Girl', again it's very tied to that bright sparkly synth sound and spanking drums, but within its realm, it's good stuff, and again, it's highly sing-along-able.

'Dum Dum Girl' (US Mix)

The differences between the UK and US mix might seem very minor to the average admirer, but some people have to have/hear absolutely everything.

'It's Getting Late In The Evening'

The B-side of 'Life Is What You Make It', to many, this will seem like simply mucking around in the studio, but it's valuable as a kind of work-in-progress document for anyone who loves *The Colour Of Spring*. As one observer put it, these are 'wonderful fragments of the experimental sessions'. The main instrument is piano, with Mark's tentative vocals feeling their way, as first organ and then Variophon join the fray. Aesthetically, it's a good fit with what came next on *Spirit Of Eden*.

'For What It's Worth'

The B-side of 'Living In Another World', this features the gentle tapping of bongos, pleasant orchestral synth, piano and snaky bass, and another of Mark's exquisite vocal performances.

'Pictures Of Bernadette'

The B-side of 'Give It Up', this sports a dirty chorus organ riff that's pure '60s garage rock, and like its A-side, has a groove that just won't give up. It works.

'Eden' (Edit)

And suddenly, we're in a brand new world, that of *Spirit Of Eden*. What a shift in time and space. It's somewhat pointless listening to an edit of this great song when the group itself didn't feel a single was necessary and released it under record company pressure.

'John Cope'

The B-side of 'I Believe In You', this is another mood-enhanced piece with a shuffle beat, some almost Californian hippy-era guitar and groovy, twinkling keyboards, it's an oddly beatific track and Mark gives it just enough.

The Collection (2000)

Released in 2000, *The Collection* is simply another EMI ploy to squeeze more cash out of the cow. There was no band involvement. The album has been reissued at various times with slightly different titles, like *It's My Life: The Collection* (2001), *The Ultra Selection* (2001) and simply, *The Collection* (2003). The song selection and running order could have been devised by a computer. The choices are just weird, and even a Spotify auto-generator could figure out a more appropriate selection of top tracks. You can do so much better.

'Talk Talk'
'It's My Life'
'Without You'
'Strike Up The Band'
'Life's What You Make It'
'It's Getting Late In The Evening'
'Pictures Of Bernadette'
'Happiness Is Easy'
'The Last Time'
'I Don't Believe In You'
'It's You'
'Talk Talk' (demo)
'It's So Serious'
'The Party's Over'
'Candy'

Missing Pieces (2001)

Personnel:
Mark Hollis: vocal, guitar, piano, organ
Lee Harris: drums
Mark Feltham: harmonica
Martin Ditcham: percussion
Tim Fries Green: organ, piano, harmonium
Levine Andrade: viola
Stephen Tees: viola
George Robertson: viola
Gavyn Write: viola
Jack Glickman: viola
Garfield Jackson: viola
Wilf Gilbson: viola
Simon Edwards: acoustic bass
Ernest Mothie: acoustic bass
Rodger Smith: cello
Paul Kegg: cello

Henry Lowther: trumpet, flugelhorn
Dave White: contrabass clarinet

Missing Pieces is a 2001 compilation of mostly *Laughing Stock* A-sides and
B-sides that, sadly, barely justifies its existence. I had thought that because
it was released on engineer Phill Brown's Pond Life label, it might constitute
an insight on the last version of Talk Talk that we couldn't quite get from
the album itself, as the final product was so finely tuned and controlled. But
of the seven tracks, only two of them feature pieces not otherwise available
(unless you happen to have the B-sides).

The remaining songs are more-or-less identical to the album tracks, but
they don't sound as good: it's as if the sparkle and depth has been somehow
taken off the recordings, whether by poor mastering or inferior sources.

It's a desultory affair with unusually poor James Marsh artwork and a
paucity of information about the tracks, which is a great pity. The digipack
version includes musician credits, but the jewel box version doesn't.

In his book, *Are We Still Rolling?,* Phill details the ways in which Mark and
the others repeatedly made promises that they didn't keep (financial ones,
as fallouts are almost always about money), and I can't help wondering
whether, in some small way, Phill subconsciously saw this album as a way of
recouping his losses.

'After The Flood' (A-side outtake)

Theoretically an outtake from the album, this version of 'After The Flood'
varies little from the album version. It sounds a little more chaotic and less
cohesive to the version we know and love, with less space in the mix and
less evident care in the mix of sounds coming through.

'Myrrhman' (B-side)

Great song, but what do we benefit from hearing it here, as opposed to the
album? Of interest only to those who want to hear the single A's and B's in
sequence.

'New Grass' (A-side)

How did all nine minutes fit on a single? Once again, if it's substantially
different to the album version, this humble reviewer certainly couldn't pick it.

'Stump' (B-side)

A B-side that wasn't on *Laughing Stock*, this is definitely worth hearing
as it's a rare example of the band improvising in the studio. There are
scratchy acoustic guitar noises a la Derek Bailey and Kraut rock-style drums,
wiggly electric guitar, feedback drone and random noises. It's like a bad
acid flashback with ominous noises in the outro. I'd love to have some
information on this track, as we have been told over and over again that no

surplus material exists from the last two official albums, and that everything not used on *Laughing Stock* was deleted. Was this something they were working on and rejected or simply a weird jam that went nowhere?

'Ascension Day' (A-side)
Same as the album, more or less.

'5:09' (B-side)
A B-side that wasn't on *Laughing Stock*. Another one that's worth hearing as it's quite a stand-alone piece that sounds nothing like the album. It's ambient, watery, with echoed melodica and backwards tape.

'Piano'
'Piano' is from Phill's *AV1* album under the name Allinson/Brown. It was supposedly for an art exhibition. It's really just 15 minutes of some guy (supposedly Mark) sitting at a piano mucking around with the sustain pedal on; pleasant enough, but hardly classic Hollis, and not actually even Talk Talk. The *AV1* album itself is a rather lovely example of atmospheric ambient music (see description later on).

Introducing... Talk Talk (2003)
Yet another fairly pointless EMI squeezing of the proverbial teat, the 2003 compilation *Introducing... Talk Talk* was useful only for those who didn't already own *Asides Besides*, as both replicate the previously rare single B-sides, 'Call In The Night Boy' (Piano Version), 'For What It's Worth', 'It's Getting Late In The Evening' and 'John Cope'.

'Have You Heard The News?'
'Candy'
'Renee'
'Tomorrow Started'
'Call In The Night Boy' (Piano Version)
'For What It's Worth'
'Happiness Is Easy'
'April 5th'
'It's Getting Late In The Evening'
'Desire'
'John Cope'
'I Believe In You'

Essential (2011)
This 2011 collection is – as the title suggests – a collecting together of the Talk Talk songs that everyone wants to hear. It's a predictable but

reasonable selection that would work on any digital jukebox but has nothing new to offer.

'Talk Talk'
'Today'
'Have You Heard The News'
'My Foolish Friend'
'Dum Dum Girl'
'Such A Shame'
'It's My Life'
'Tomorrow Started'
'Happiness Is Easy'
'Life's What You Make It'
'Living In Another World'
'Give It Up'
'Eden'
'Desire'
'I Believe In You'

Natural Order 1982-1991 (2013)

By 2013, no one was expecting any new material from Mark Hollis. After all, he put his career to bed way back in the late '90s, and apart from a few false starts and half-hearted contributions to other people's projects, there was a profound silence. That he would come out of self-imposed seclusion to curate yet another Talk Talk collection seems like a fiction, but it happened.

Billed as a companion piece to *Natural History – The Very Best Of Talk Talk, Natural Order* is a kind of oppositional document to that earlier compilation, which contains few of the well-known songs, and for the first time, includes tracks from their one post-EMI album, *Laughing Stock*.

According to the record company bumf, Mark not only curated the tracklisting, but also the running order, mastering and artwork. Clearly, Mark's choice is not completely based on artistic motives, but was more personal, with room for a little nostalgia.

'Have You Heard The News?
'Renée'
'For What It's Worth'
'Chameleon Day'
'April 5th'
'Wealth'
'John Cope'
'Eden'
'After The Flood' (Alternative Version)
'Taphead'

Live Talk Talk

Spend any time on Talk Talk fan pages and you'll come away with the impression that Mark Hollis practically walks on water. This is fairly common on band and artist sites, where any kind of critical assessment is typically bludgeoned to death by slavish and ardent adulation. There will always be fans who insist that the worst album is, in fact, fantastic. As for Talk Talk as a live outfit, it's easy to find the more religious of Mark's fans who consider the group's concert appearances as a manifestation of the second coming.

The truth is more troublesome. The group accrued a sizable trove of middling-to-poor reviews of their gigs between 1981 and 1986, after which, like The Beatles before them, they ceased to function as a performing group and put their creative energies into their albums. Adoring fans, meanwhile, have fond memories of the concerts they attended, but their assessments are hardly dispassionate. The rest of us have scant evidence to go on, because Talk Talk didn't release any live albums during their short reign, and subsequently, there's only been one proper live CD and one live DVD. And while there are random 'live in studio' and a few other live shows to be found on mediums like YouTube, they're typically of dubious visual and/or sonic quality.

We know that Mark, who, as the singer, was undoubtedly the front person and, therefore, the visual focus, suffered some kind of anxiety disorder and hated thousands of eyes trained on him while he sang. We also know that he considered the recording studio to be his real stage. It was the one place he could dictate the terms, and work towards creating whatever it was he'd heard in his head. He's been quoted on several occasions talking about how he felt that live shows were a trial, because they involved repeating, parrot-fashion, over and over, songs that he'd already perfected in a recording studio. In that sense, he was more like a painter than a musician/performer.

Live shows at their best aren't merely a copy-cat exposition of an existent studio recording, but something else: partly a communion between audience and artist, partly a chance for band and audience to get their yah-yah's out; but most importantly, they're an opportunity for the musicians to show how they gel as a band, and how they can stretch out and become one, 'in the moment'. It seems that Talk Talk were never comfortable with any of that. Undoubtedly, Paul and Lee were a superb rhythm unit, but without genuine collusion from the singer/leader, the sonic transport of a great live event cannot occur.

For now, at least, the only official examples we have of Talk Talk in concert are a couple of gigs recorded in the wake of *The Colour Of Spring* in 1986, one a CD and one a DVD. And while they're essential for completists, they both feel less than the sum of their parts.

London 1986 (1998)
Personnel:
Mark Hollis: vocals
Paul Webb: bass and vocals

Lee Harris: drums
David Rhodes: guitar and vocals
Danny Cummins: percussion
Phil Reis: percussion
Ian Curnow: keyboards
Rupert Black: piano
Mark Feltham: harmonica

Recorded on 8 May 1986, at the Hammersmith Odeon near the end of a European tour to promote the then-current album, *The Colour Of Spring*, the setlist only includes three tunes from that album, 'Life's What You Make It' (or 'Life Is What You Make It', according to the tracklist), 'Living In Another World' and 'Give It Up'. It's hard to fathom the reason for this, given Mark's ongoing determination to do it his way, to keep on moving forward, and not look back. Perhaps the setlist was a rare compromise to ensure that the audience got what they came for (unlikely), or perhaps they simply weren't ready to perform more material from such a musically detailed and somewhat complex album (likely).

London 1986 wouldn't see the light of day until 1998, the same year that Mark released his first and only solo album. Like the mostly *Laughing Stock*-based collection of odds and sods, *Missing Pieces*, it was released on engineer Phill Brown's short-lived Pond Life label. A mere eight songs over less than an hour's running time, the album feels perfunctory. What possessed Phill to release the album? He'd fallen out with Mark over money matters subsequent to the recording of his solo album, and previous to that, had fallen out with Paul and Lee, with whom he'd worked on the 'O'Rang project. Was *London 1986* all about clawing some of his lost income back?

Apparently recorded by Tim and Mick McKenna and mixed by Phill, it has to be said that *London 1986* is a middling set that isn't up to the band's usual audio standards, although it's substantially better sounding than a bootleg recording.

The last gig they ever performed in the UK, it comes across as rather tired and feels like an anonymous set of studio musicians backing a really great singer on a set of great songs. And the 'guests' so important to *The Colour Of Spring* are mostly missing in action: the ever-reliable David Rhodes is aboard, as is Mark Feltham and his diatonic harmonica, but important contributors to the 1986 group like Martin Ditcham, Morris Pert, Danny Thompson, Robbie McIntosh and Steve Winwood are not there. It's immediately apparent that despite his fear of performing, however, Mark's vocal performances are reliably superb. But the question remains: why would anyone want to listen to this when the studio performances are leagues ahead in every respect?

'Tomorrow Started'

There's audience hubbub, then a Satie-esque introduction on electric piano and a little synth, which is still very forward in the mix when the band

comes in. Some idiots in the audience are yelling out just as Mark starts
singing. Instantly, his vocal presence transforms what otherwise pretty much
just sounds like a bunch of jobbing session musos. Amazingly, his singing
is every bit as good as the studio, but the recording of it is just average.
In many ways, this sounds like the earlier band, not the band we love. A
strangely low-key, morbidly depressing note to begin on.

'Life's What You Make It'
This song had been a hit just five months earlier, so it's exceptionally well-
received. Mark's voice sounds good, but the limitations of the microphone
are obvious. He gets it so perfectly up close in the studio that it's impossible
to perfectly replicate onstage. David Rhodes makes a fair stab at the song's
signature guitar figure, but it's not quite right, and he fails to replicate its tone
and especially, the precise bending of the melody. There's a going-through-
the-motions vibe that can't be dispelled. It's hard to say what it sounded like
on the night, but it's disappointing to hear a humdrum performance of the
song, which lacks the sonic splendour of the studio recording.

'Does Caroline Know?'
An oldie with the South American flute setting on synth making it seem
rather cheesy. In fact, it sounds rather like a backing track for about two
minutes until Mark comes in. The band's performance is listless and Mark's
voice has a harsh, metallic edge. And boy, it does go on! Not much happens
except for a wee bit of a piano solo, the drums ticking away, and a hint of
conga.

'Living In Another World'
Once again, a song that would have been a hit just a few months before
seems to drag and go on for ages. As a reproduction of the recorded artefact,
it's like a photocopy or a lo-res file. Everything is where it's supposed to be
– the keyboard orchestra, the organ, Feltham's harmonica – but it just never
distinguishes itself.

'Give It Up'
This song works, because, at last, there's some heat and motion on a song
that's as close as the band ever got to gospel music. Mark sounds a bit unsure
at the beginning, before launching into the anthemic 'got to give it up' with
its exultant organ surge. Up until now, the setlist has seemed weighed down
and at last the audience are given some positive energy to clap along to.

'It's My Life'
In realisation that this is the part of the performance the audience needs to
kick up its heels, the group build a percussion solo into the song with congas
and a big drum sound.

'Such A Shame'

After a slightly strange beginning, the song-proper starts and the Joy Division meets Spector classic pop aspect is highlighted. The performance is a little rough, but Mark's voice is splendid.

'Renee'

Naturally, Talk Talk end their show with a downer ballad. Go home, everyone.

Live At Montreux 1986 (2008)

Personnel:
Mark Hollis: lead vocals
Paul Webb: bass, backing vocals
Lee Harris: drums
John Turnbull: guitars, backing vocals
Ian Curnow: synthesizers, organ, piano, programming
Rupert Black: synthesizers, electric piano, drum machine
Phil Reis: percussion
Leroy Williams: percussion

Released on DVD in 2008 at a time when Eagle Vision was issuing a whole swag of historic Montreux Jazz Festival performances, *Live At Montreux* was recorded on 11 July 1986 during the last leg of the European tour supporting *The Colour Of Spring.*

It's interesting to note that several of the musicians featured on *Live 1986,* recorded just two months previously, have been replaced: most notably David Rhodes (John Turnbull) and Danny Cummins (Leroy Williams).

The fact that it was released a long 22 years after the concert took place speaks volumes. The only official live performance by Talk Talk released outside of the *London 1986* (released 1998) CD from the same tour; it's a sometimes painful reminder of Mark's reticence to perform and inability (or unwillingness) to entertain a crowd.

While the group assembled for the tour are professional and replicate the songs with a fair degree of skill, there's a certain anonymity that pervades the whole thing. No wonder that this was amongst the last concerts ever by the group.

While they hadn't reached the level of meticulous layering that came with *Spirit Of Eden,* the songs on the then-current album *The Colour Of Spring* were rendered with such exactitude and perfection on the album itself that a live performance of an album that was never really geared to be played live simply can't match the recorded version. Not that they performed many songs from it, preferring instead to chart a course through some of the better songs from their catalogue up to that time. Of course, I'll meet a lot of resistance from hardcore Talk Talk fans who thought every single thing they ever did was amazing. But compare any of these in-performance versions with the albums they came from, and you'll see what I mean.

A few surprising things, then. It's surprising how animated Mark seems, and it's surprising how emotional and pitch-perfect his oration is. But in contrast to both the honesty and accuracy of Mark's performance, the band often just seem so beige, and they don't ever really feel like a group, more a bunch of hired guns, which answers my question about why they don't seem to quite fit together, visually, aesthetically, or musically.

Still, in comparison to the *London 1986 CD*, *Live At Montreux 1986* is a blast. It sounds fairly good, and while the overall presentation is professional enough, there's nothing flashy about the camera work or the stage set. And that's a good thing.

'Talk Talk'
Percussionist Leroy Williams (formerly of Level 42) is already shirtless and adding onstage energy and charisma with his shaker. The audience is enthusiastic and clustered up right near the lip of the stage. Mark wears an '80s ponytail, which dates the event more than the music. It's an odd match visually, with guitarist John Turnbull (Dave Stewart & The Spiritual Cowboys) looking like a reject from a metal band, Paul bopping up and down with his short, floppy, fringe-laced '80s cut, and keyboardist Ian Curnow looking like an escapee from an accordion group. Second keyboardist Rupert Black (RIP), has a more distinguished, scholarly look. Mark is fairly animated behind the imagined protection of his sunglasses.

'Dum Dum Girl'
It must have been a hot night, as Lee already has his shirt off by song number two. John plays acoustic guitar and Paul gets to do his Mick Karn fretless bass thing.

'Call In The Night Boy'
Why even play this song? It's so reflective of their earlier stuff, but enthusiastically played nevertheless, with an almost Kraut beat and wiggly guitar lead. The group get to kick out the jams a little with some drum and bass work and piano soloing that's not on the original cut.

'Tomorrow Started'
This song led off the *London 1986 CD* with its Satie-esque piano. You can clearly hear the added percussion and Mellotron-like orchestral synth. While John performs on acoustic guitar, what sounds like an electric guitar is actually the synth. The audience looks a bit jaded, having to deal with a slow song they can't bop to. Mark flops his fringe regularly, as if to emphasise certain words.

'My Foolish Friend'

This is an opportunity for John to wig out and do his dirty guitar hero thing. It's a bit of an indulgence and doesn't feel entirely appropriate in this context.

'Life's What You Make It'

And finally, we get a between-song utterance from Mark, in which he states that it's a track from the new album. John's handling of the guitar melody is closer to the recorded version than Robbie's on the *London 1986 CD*, but it doesn't have the bite of the original version, and neither does the drum sound. It's odd how Mark bops his head up and down like a budgie.

'Mirror Man/Does Caroline Know?'

There's voice, keyboard, piano, and then drums and that Andean flute effect on the synth. A choir too? Where's that coming from? There's quite a bit of space for the instruments to play in, and another amusing faked guitar solo on synth, then a piano solo, and prominent congas. Mark extemporises into the mike at the end.

'It's You'

One of the least impressive Talk Talk songs gets a workout. What a strange choice. Rupert Williams goes a little crazy with his cymbals.

'Chameleon Day/Living In Another World'

They seem to have discovered the idea of smashing several songs together. There are two guitar solos, which is two too many, really. 'Living In Another World TO YOU!' Mark emphasises. He cuts a strange figure. When he's singing, he's all teeth. He is surprisingly active in movement, but it's mostly his head.

'Give It Up'

The audience is frenzied at this point. This song sounds a bit 'off' at the start, just the way it did on the *London 1986 CD*, so it can't have been an accident. Nice that they could more or less replicate Winwood's fruity organ. There's just something too polite and gentrified about this blue-eyed gospel in a live context, but the crowd lap it up and clap it up. There's yet more synth-guitar!

'It's My Life'

There's organ, acoustic guitar, and those ship's horn synth notes. There's even a conga-based percussion solo. Mark's vocal performance (and performances plural) are powerful. He says goodnight.

'I Don't Believe In You'

The first encore, and of course, rather than risk ramping up the audience, Mark chooses a slow song. There's a random hum and another amusing fake guitar solo.

'Such A Shame'

Those crazy synth sounds at the start, and acoustic guitar again. Rupert bangs away on a tambourine, and there's a bit of an acoustic guitar solo. Mark says goodnight again, again.

'Renee'

The second encore. The crowd claps along to the instrumental part, which sounds wrong because it's such a quiet song, with a hushed, almost Japan-type feel, aside from Mark's distinctive voice. The audience gets out their lighters. Sigh. At the end, Mark says: 'Thank you very much, thank you very much. Good night. God bless. Thank you very much'. And slopes off. He's *such an* unlikely pop star.

Talk Talk On Film

Natural History: The Best Of Talk Talk – A Video Selection (1990)

It goes without saying that Talk Talk are not especially well represented in the televisual realm. Easily the best video capture of the live band – such as it was – is *Live At Montreux 1986*. There are a few other live appearances to be found on YouTube, but they're really only of archaeological interest. You can drive yourself nuts with the endless vacuity of European TV show appearances, by the end of which you'll be empathising with Mark and drawing the same conclusions he did. Or you can search vainly for interviews, where Mark reveals little and is often either evasive or stops short of fully articulating his thoughts. And then there are the actual, official video clips. Oh, dear. We all know how dated and terribly time-stamped 1980s video clips seem today, forgetting that at the time, MTV was new and revolutionary and we looked forward week by week with great anticipation to seeing the latest video clips on 'the box'.

Unfortunately, time hasn't been as kind to the video medium as it has to music recordings. Bands and artists who insisted on celluloid rather than videotape have fared slightly better, because video back then was just such a low-res medium, and today's hi-res televisions reveal its limitations. Then there are the often ham-struck, cheesy concepts that video directors lumbered bands with. The best video clips from the era tend to be the ones that didn't take themselves too seriously: Talking Heads and Devo being two great examples. Talk Talk weren't a visually oriented band, and their visual identity was, for all intents and purposes, James Marsh's iconic artwork. They lacked the visual panache of Duran Duran and their ilk, so video was never going to be a perfect match.

But if approached with all that in mind, the group's small selection of video clips – brought together in 1990 on the companion piece to the *Natural History: The Best Of Talk Talk CD* – is fairly entertaining. (Note: In 2007, this VCR video compilation was reissued as a DVD to accompany the CD compilation.)

'Today'

The filming and editing techniques on display here are even more dated than the song itself. We see a boy getting out of bed, and Mark driving around in a car.

'Talk Talk' (Version One)

The official version has the band members faffing around and playing silly buggers on a shiny set. It's kind of embarrassing but a little bit fun, too.

'Talk Talk' (Version Two)

This 'alternative mix' is so very 1982, with the group wearing their EMI-sanctioned white suits and thin ties. There's certainly no confusing these guys with Duran Duran! If you can stem the embarrassment (hey, we're laughing with them, not at them, okay?), this is once again fairly entertaining.

'My Foolish Friend'
What were they thinking? It's as though they saw a Ken Loach film about industrial England and got inspired to incorporate the working class theme into their own video clip. This is factory life, with Mark simply wandering around the streets.

'Such A Shame'
This clip is surprisingly good, and it's nice to see close-ups of a fresh-faced Mark smiling, with an expressive face. It must have been weird for fans encountering the visage of this unlikely-looking pop star for the first time. The jokiness of the clip is at odds with the melancholy tenor of the song and his voice, which makes for a refreshing contrast.

'Dum Dum Girl' (Take 1)
Another rather excellent, revealing clip in which we find the band standing around in a field chatting about how silly they feel making the video. They make a mockery of pretend-singing-in-a-field and it's fun to get a small insight into the band's sense of humour and repartee.

'Dum Dum Girl' (Take 2)
The actual clip of the band miming the tune on a field lacks the madcap humour of the 'making of' version.

'It's My Life' (UK Version)
It's not clear why they filmed this at a zoo, but it makes for a rather odd, interesting clip; especially given the fact that Mark is filmed with various animal/enclosure backdrops *not* miming to the song, and the rest of the band are missing in action.

'Life's What You Make It'
Like the other video clips from *The Colour Of Spring,* this is pretty good, all things considered. The group are captured outside at night in a natural setting, performing in near-darkness: with piano and simple drum kit the props.

'Living In Another World'
Another dark, night-time clip and it's a beauty, featuring just Mark and a piano, and when he sings the 'Help me...' line bright lights come on and a gale blows. There's a lot of close-up head-shaking going on, and at one point, he's even suspended upside down. Funny/bizarre.

'Give It Up'

This is supposedly a video clip, but it's actually a live performance – or at least, looks like it. Nicely filmed.

'I Believe In You'

The last video clip that Mark would ever endure and even though he had a say over its content and concept, later, he was quoted as saying he regretted doing it and that he felt like he had prostituted himself. I think most Talk Talk fans will have a kinder perspective. It's simple, with one long shot of Mark that is occasionally superimposed with other band members. The only real change during its length is the gradations of light on Mark's face.

After Talk Talk – Solo & Collaborative Projects
Mark Hollis

Mark Hollis (1998)

Personnel:
Mark Hollis – vocals, guitar
Martin Ditcham – drums, percussion
Chris Laurence – double bass
Lawrence Pendrous – piano, harmonium
Iain Dixon – clarinet
Tim Holmes – clarinet
Mark Feltham – harmonica
Henry Lowther – trumpet
Andy Panayi – flute
Melinda Maxwell – cor anglais
Dominic Miller – guitar
Robbie McIntosh – guitar
Maggie Pollock – bassoon
Julie Andrews – bassoon
Produced at Master Rock Studios, by Mark Hollis.
Engineered by Phill Brown.
UK release date: 26 January 1998.
Highest chart places: UK: 19
Running time: 46:56

It's not surprising that *Mark Hollis* sounds more like a last gasp than a record announcing the promising beginning of a solo career: it was supposed to be a Talk Talk album, fulfilment of the two-album Polydor contract. But where to go after *Laughing Stock,* an album that sounded like the end point of a journey? The last track on that album, 'Runeii', felt like a literal dissolution of the elements that made the group, a psychic fragmentation that would be impossible to reassemble.

Mark Hollis attempts to write a new chapter by taking a different approach to instrumentation, eschewing the rock group entirely for a mostly acoustic approach that sounded more like a small orchestra. Some hailed this as pure genius, and on its 1998 release, many of the post-rock musicians inspired by *Spirit Of Eden* and *Laughing Stock* were enamoured by Mark's conviction to welcome even more space and an overwhelming quietude.

Those with the patience for its discrete tones thought it brilliant, while others felt the absence of Lee's pulse and the dynamic variation of the previous two albums. For many – including this writer – *Mark Hollis* was a step too far. Yes, it's a very good album, but for the most part, his vocals, his lyrical obsessions, and the overall tone hadn't changed; and deprived of the grooves and the break-out drama of the noisy bits on the previous two albums, there was little tension-and-release. For the first time, there was little to deflect or balance Mark's gloomy attitude. It was tempting to suggest that he needed to take a happy pill.

As it was, it had taken seven long years for Mark to find the stamina to fulfil that Polydor contract, despite a million-dollar advance that many musicians would have been over the moon about. Understandably, after the intense and not entirely happy experience of recording *Laughing Stock*, the core Talk Talk team had needed time apart. But while Mark was keen to continue working with Tim and Phill, they'd both had enough and by the mid-'90s, they weren't talk-talking at all.

It's worth taking a moment to consider the working relationship. As a musical dilettante, Mark needed collaborators to make something of his ideas. Presumably, he valued these working relationships, but the value he placed on the individuals he worked with never translated into being treated with respect commensurate with their creative input or rewarded adequately from a monetary perspective. Mark clearly expected total commitment from Tim, Lee and Phill during the recording of both *Spirit Of Eden* and *Laughing Stock*. The commitment required, and the length of time each project took, was almost cult-like.

In rock lore, perhaps the classic example of cult-like behaviour was that of Captain Beefheart and his Magic Band during the famously punishing extended rehearsals of the iconic *Trout Mask Replica* album. Like Mark, Don Van Vliet (Captain Beefheart) was essentially a dilettante with a great set of pipes and some exceptionally original ideas that he needed his musicians to realise.

During the six months or so in which the band created and rehearsed the material for the album, Don was often cruel to his band members, almost never acknowledging their contributions, and leading to allegations of a cult-like atmosphere and abusive relationships.

It may be going a step too far to claim abusive, manipulative behaviour during the *Spirit Of Eden* and *Laughing Stock* sessions, but Mark's core team didn't get to have lives for almost a year at a time, and what's more, they were immersed in such a strange environment that it left psychological scars on its participants, ruining several marriages in the process and necessitating psychological counselling. Why would Tim, Phill and Lee give so much of themselves for what for all intents and purposes, was Mark's project? Undoubtedly, they were being paid to do a job, but that doesn't explain their full immersion. They clearly felt burned afterwards, however, which explains their reticence to work with Mark again.

Conjecture is fairly pointless, but the statements Phill and Tim have both made about their need to distance themselves from Mark gives us a perspective on what happened next. What did happen was that over the years subsequent to *Laughing Stock*, Mark cast around for new collaborators without ever finding the perfect match.

He tried working on his own and figured out how to write some arrangements for woodwind, but knew that he would need to work with others to get an album together. Ultimately, he would work with several random individuals over the course of the next few years, and while it would eventually yield the *Mark Hollis* album, few of those collaborators ended up feeling happy with the treatment they received. Writing partners on the album would include former Talk Talk session keyboardist Phil Ramocon, former Sting guitarist Dominic Miller, classically trained schoolteacher Laurence Pendrous and engineer/producer Warne Livesey.

Manager Keith Aspden recommended former The The engineer/producer Livesy, who would write five of the eight songs with Mark. Warne and Mark worked together in each other's houses for about two years. 'It was a unique, often frustrating, but ultimately rewarding experience', said Warne. 'The entire record was scored exactly, with the exception of the solos. He was very focused on every minute detail. When we were scoring parts, there would be timing intricacies that were written down to the $1/64^{th}$ of a beat'.

Unfortunately, the two fell out over a big misunderstanding: Warne thought the compositions they were working on and recording as they went were the actual album, but to Mark, they were merely demos, a practice run.

Studio time was booked and Mark asked Phill to engineer the album, but he refused. 'I didn't want to do any more recording with Mark because of the stress of it', said Phill in his memoir, *Are We Still Rolling?*. Phill did, however, set up the gear the way Mark wanted it, with a couple of old microphones and lots of room ambience. Three months of recording then took place before Mark had a good listen to the results, and was shocked to hear that it sounded all wrong. Despite Phill's instructions, the instruments had been close mic'd, and the room ambience had been lost in the process. At this point, Phill finally bowed to Mark's pressure, and returned to salvage the project.

The idea was to re-record only certain performances, but they ended up erasing around 40 per cent of the album. The studio bill for the first, largely wasted three months, was 100 thousand pounds.

The sessions are said to have been much more relaxed than those of *Laughing Stock.* Mark was amenable and there was no mucking about with psychedelic lighting effects. There were, however, some odd decisions made and a few strange incidents. For some reason, expensive superstar drummers Steve Gadd and Vinnie Colaiuta were both brought in at some point and instructed to perform dead-simple stick work. Mark said the feel was all wrong and got Martin Ditcham to replace their parts.

By November 1997, they had begun final overdubs, and by December, the Talk Talk album *Mountains Of The Moon* was ready to mix. Initial preview cassettes of the album were sent out with both the band name and the album title, but Mark had been thinking. It was always supposed to be a Talk Talk album, but Mark was the sole remaining member. It made more sense for the album to go out under his own name.

Unsurprisingly, Polydor was less than enamoured with how they'd spent their million dollars. Those sympathetic to Talk Talk at the label had all gone, and there was a new team there with hits on their minds and little use for acts that defied easy pigeon-holing. But at least under the Talk Talk banner, the album would sell to certified fans. Who even knew who this 'Mark Hollis' was? Polydor would release the album, but do almost nothing to promote it, and there would be no video. It's hard to imagine Mark being surprised or disappointed, as he'd already announced his intention never to make another video clip, and not to tour.

Surprisingly, Mark also chose not to use a James Marsh painting, instead opting for a rather obscure black and white photograph of Easter bread designed to look like The Lamb of God. This gave the sleeve a look somewhat similar to that of the German label ECM, of which he was a fan, but it lacked the glacial beauty of the typical ECM cover art.

The album was finally released on 26 January 1998. It got great reviews but sold poorly, spending only one week on the UK charts. (It would be reissued several times, most recently by Universal in 2019).

One of the few extensive interviews Mark conducted to promote the album was with Rob Young of *The Wire* magazine, in which he expresses an admiration for the work of Robert Wyatt, says that he hates the glorification of drugs, and sums up his attitude and approach to lyrics by expressing his admiration for the made-up language of Can's Damo Suzuki. (Mark erroneously names Can's other singer, Malcolm Mooney, but that's beside the point).

Mark is said to have known that *Mark Hollis* would be his last album, and that he was realistic that without major label funding, he could not make the kind of albums he wanted.

Apart from a couple of guest shots, the album would be the last we would ever hear from Mark. He was enticed into a cameo appearance on UNKLE's 'Chaos' (1998) but hated the way his contribution was mixed and appeared under the John Cope pseudonym. He played piano on Phill Brown's 1998 *AV* instrumental album. He contributed to Anja Garbarek's *Smiling & Waving* (2001), although his plan to produce the album didn't work out. Over the years, several projects, including film scores, were discussed but always thwarted. In 2004 he started work on a film score for Sofia Coppola's *Marie Antoinette* film, but she changed her mind, opting to use punk classics instead. Similarly, he made some music for a Wim Wenders film in 2014, but it wasn't what Wim wanted. Many musicians and groups – including Radiohead – expressed interest in working with Mark, but the enthusiasm wasn't reciprocated.

Mark certainly had little financial incentive to work. In 2005 and 2006, Hollis Songs made a small fortune off the back of No Doubt's hit cover of 'It's My Life' and renewed interest in Talk Talk via compilations, and Mark is said to have poured that cash into his passion for Ducati motorcycles. The Hollis family regularly travelled, and Mark enjoyed following football and riding on long motorcycle expeditions. (In 2012, he shipped his bike to the US and rode the Trans-America Trail.)

Mark Feltham, who became a family friend, remarked about two curious things: That Mark would never talk about music, and that his house was always incredibly tidy. It makes sense that he would compartmentalise. The supreme effort that went into the last two Talk Talk albums speaks volumes about Mark's ability to focus and give his all to whatever he was doing at the time. That he was a clean freak is, on reflection, unsurprising. After all, someone with his degree of musical vision, who could 'paint' the various threads of a composition together in the unique way he did on the last three albums, is likely to be obsessive over detail in their personal life, too.

In 2018 close friends of Mark were told that he had late-stage cancer. He died in February 2019. The exact date of his death has never been revealed.

'The Colour Of Spring'

The only song co-written with session keyboardist Phil Ramocon – who had performed with Talk Talk in concert and on *It's My Life* – 'The Colour Of Spring' starts with a prolonged silence, like a silent prayer. It's an extremely intimate-sounding and rather brief song featuring just Mark's tremulous, soulful vocal and the piano skills of school music teacher Lawrence Pendrous, with whom Mark had struck up a friendship.

The recording has plenty of tape hiss and the sound of the piano is muted, as if it was performed in a drawing room with a microphone in the adjoining hallway. The initial simple piano chords have a religious feeling similar to those of Paul McCartney's 'Let It Be', but then there's a gorgeous descending figure that sounds like a fragment from an impressionist composer like Ravel or Debussy.

The lyric is a musing on the importance of living in the moment and immersing yourself in the wonder of it all rather than being consumed with the knowledge of inevitable death.

'Watershed'

Mark already sounds gone, really, on a song that seems to be about what you say to the one you love as opposed to what you mean. There is a chorus, but it doesn't sound like one and you wouldn't sing it: 'Should have said so much/Makes it harder/The more you love'. Nothing on here is catchy enough to later find yourself humming it in the shower.

The first of the five songs co-written with Warne Livesy – who, like Mark, loved the Miles Davis/Gil Evans collaborations – 'Watershed' provides the musical template for most of the others: almost entirely acoustic guitar, jingle bell drums, bass, a comforting harmonica, and wind ensemble with cor anglais or the odd touch of trumpet. The middle section features acoustic guitar strumming, double bass and trumpet, with light jazz-oriented drums.

'Inside Looking Out'

The only song composed solely by Mark, the lyrics of 'Inside Looking Out' read almost like an old blues song: 'Feel my skin Lord/Feel my luck tumbling down/Left no life no more'. But he sings those words in an utterly devastated voice that perhaps has a deeper connection to ancient folk heritage.

The track begins with a ruminative piano section before the strummed guitar and voice enters, along with bass, miscellaneous room sounds (shuffling, creaking) and eventually, harmonium ... signalling the piano's return.

'The Gift'

Another co-composition with Warne Livesey, 'The Gift' appears to be an observation about someone once pure but now burnt out and shamed. 'So sold out... How on earth did you come to live as a clown' he sings in that same haunted, devastated voice.

Mark Ditcham achieves a groove here that's close enough to Lee's shuffling on *Laughing Stock* (sans the louder percussives) to create some welcome sonic connective tissue. Chris Lawrence's bass lines help, too. There's also a little intentionally rudimentary acoustic guitar, a harmonica solo and a few woodwinds.

'A Life (1895-1915)'

A rare example of a historical event inspiring Mark in song, 'A Life (1895-1915)' – a bit of an epic at eight minutes and 10 seconds – refers to a soldier and poet, Roland Leighton, who was only 20 years old when killed in the First World War. Mark appears to have been fascinated by the patriotism that led so many young men to death, and presumably read an account of Leighton by his former fiancée, a nurse who became a pacifist after the war.

Musically, Mark is said to have been influenced on this track (and on 'The Daily Planet') by early 20th-century composer Schoenberg, whose 12-tone system revolutionised (and scandalised) the classical world. Perhaps this is one of the pieces for woodwind that Mark was working on years before the album came together – a small wind ensemble of clarinet, flute, cor anglais and bassoon joined by bass and voice.

This is as close as Mark ever got to constructing a prog masterpiece and it rivals one of Mark's favourites, Kate Bush, and her 'Seventh Wave' suite for its ability to transport the listener.

While it begins and ends with the austere sound of the wind ensemble, the middle section establishes a delicate piano vamp, a hypnotic beat and what sounds like a very quiet French girls' chorus. (These singers are uncredited, though Phill reckons they were 'four women whispering'). Mark's vocals are sublime, and their skilful manipulation summons up the spirit of Tim Buckley in one of his more somnolent moods. Altogether, the elements make for one of the most entrancing pieces of music in the orbit of Talk Talk.

'Westward Bound'

Co-written with former Sting guitarist Dominic Miller, 'Westward Bound' came together slowly over a series of fortnightly visits to Mark's home. Miller has noted that at the end of the first session, they only had the first bar of the song – two measures – and that the song itself took as long to write as many musicians would take to write a whole album.

One of the simplest and sparest pieces on the album, Dominic plucks his acoustic in a manner redolent of a classical guitarist, but with more roughage round the edges and 'room' sound that almost becomes an instrument unto itself.

Meanwhile, Mark sings incredibly softly yet intensely. In fact, this is probably the quietest Mark ever sang on record, and the reason the air itself seems to have been picked up by the microphones. It's a song where silence is really loud. Oddly, for a song that required intensive construction, the vocal melodies – such as they are – sound almost made up on the spot.

The lyrics are definitely hard-won; however, telling a story about the birth of a child and the dedication required to nourish and raise the child, which necessitates the father take a journey to a job far away from family.

Like so many of Mark's lyrics, 'Westward Bound' cogitates around the responsibilities of adulthood, sexual union and family. Where Leonard Cohen was prone to exploring both the glory and pain of grown-up relationships in a song like 'Hallelujah', Mark's ongoing lyrical obsession was similar yet more prosaic: he's constantly attempting to resolve the paradox of life, that for everything transforming and magical and full of wonder there's an equal horror waiting to confront him on the other side of life's continuum. For Mark, in his lyrics, as in life, it was all about familial responsibility and what it takes to be a good husband and father and live an ethical life.

'The Daily Planet'

The second-to-longest track on the album at seven minutes and 19 seconds, 'The Daily Planet' seems like another lyrical delve into the contrast between the wonder of the world and all of its multifarious sins and torments. It's hard to tell whether it's also a commentary on salacious media.

The wind ensemble from 'A Life (1895-1915)' returns, soon accented by ride cymbals, shakers and acoustic bass, creating an odd mishmash that's part serial classical and part loose-limbed Coltrane-style jazz groove. Mark's vocal is much more demonstrative than the extremely hushed 'Westward Bound'. Piano, strummed guitar and a harmonica solo eventuate. Towards the end, the rhythm ceases, and Mark's voice becomes hushed, allowing for an elegiac ending.

'A New Jerusalem'

Ending on a very depressing note, father is back home with family, but he's lost the ability to love. One in five died in the war and he survived, 'But I'm dead to love/A pawn the same'.

The inference is that experiencing the horror of war deprives you of your soul, kills off your goodness, and your ability to care for your wife and kids. It's possible that he's referring not only to physical war but the war that every adult participates in to some degree, competing in the workforce, a kind of modern-day slavery.

Starting with becalmed harmonium, double bass, scratchy strummed guitar and muted piano, then one of Mark's more delicate vocals, it feels very much the end-piece, a sad goodbye. Finally, the woodwinds sing a few bars and there's a piano note on sustain ... and that's it. The album ends with the same loud silence with which it began.

Paul Webb and Lee Harris

It must have been galling for Paul and Lee, long-time friends and a hot rhythm section, to find their considerable talents sidelined in Talk Talk, as Mark took the reins and became the singular focus. Not that they had ever exhibited aspirations to lead. After all, Talk Talk had started life not as a group but as a band cobbled together to perform Mark's tunes for a demo tape. And they had obviously loved being involved not only in a group that was signed to a multinational record company but also being in a group that really felt like it was going somewhere.

Paul and Lee were proud of Talk Talk, 100 per cent behind the project, and gave it their all.

But clearly, individually, they had more to offer than playing to someone else's tune. They were still teenagers when Mark found them, and they had both matured as people and developed as musicians over the lifespan of the group.

The difficulties encountered in the making of the seminal *Spirit Of Eden* and *Laughing Stock* albums must have taken a toll on both Paul and Lee. Paul quit towards the end of *Spirit Of Eden* and wasn't around at all for *Laughing Stock*. He'd felt so sidelined by that point that it had become a humiliation. Lee had been intrinsic to the heady, heavy vibe around the recording of the albums, and it was his psychedelic lighting that had been integral to the unique mood generated. The human/machine-like drumming patterns he created were phenomenal but left him exhausted.

It took a few years for the long-time best buddies to get together again and come up with a project that would be very much Paul and Lee and Friends – 'O'Rang – but subsequent to that, neither have been exactly prolific.

Paul has certainly been active, even if his production work for other groups and artists caused a delay in the late-flowering Rustin Man project. Lee, meanwhile, while still contributing to Paul's work and taking on the odd drumming job, more or less faded from the public eye.

'O' Rang – Herd Of Instinct (1994)

Personnel:
Lee Harris: drums, percussion, vocals, harmonium, flute, bass, organ, didgeridoo, programming, editing
Paul Webb: vocals, guitar, bass, synthesizer, melodica, zurna, harmonium, organ, recorder, percussion
Simon Edwards: bass
Emily Burridge: cello
Matt Lipsey: flute
Gena Dolganov: guitar
Graham Sutton: guitar
Mark Feltham: harmonica
Matt Johnson: organ, guitar

Martin Ditcham: percussion
Anthony Thistlewaite: saxophone, mandolin
Graeme Jones: talkbox, percussion, guitar
Paul Shearsmith: trumpet, balafon
Phil Ramocon: backing vocals
Beth Gibbons: vocals
Colette Meury: vocals
Noreen Deen: vocals
Daniel Harris: voice (poem)
Produced at The Slug by Lee Harris with Phill Brown
UK release date: 25 July 1994
Running time: 44:47

When it was clear that Talk Talk was over, and they had recovered some semblance of themselves after being in Mark's thrall for so many years, the pair embarked on a project that would take a great leap into the unknown and allow them to assert their musical magic within a conceptual framework that was even headier than anything their former group had ever done.

After the snail-like progress and excessive demands of Talk Talk, their new project must have felt like heavenly-scented freedom. The new group, it turned out, wouldn't simply be a postscript to Talk Talk but something utterly, compellingly unique. For many, their two albums would continue to elude comprehension into the 21st century, but others saw them as shining beacons of adventurous musical fusion.

While Mark and Tim created a kind of fusion on the last two Talk Talk albums, theirs was very specific, and very controlled. There was Mark's love of the albums Miles Davis made with orchestrator Gil Evans, together with his increasing interest in 20th-century classical music, not to mention the blue-eyed soul that oozed out in his singing. Paul and Lee's project, however, would use an exotic range of instruments to project a world music atmosphere. Just as surprising was their absorption of influences from the new British dance music underground, although it pays not to forget that when Mark discovered them, they were playing in a dub-reggae group, so they were never groove-averse.

There were ways in which Talk Talk and 'O'Rang were similar – their propensity for experimentation, their quintessential Englishness – but they were also poles apart, stylistically and aesthetically. It's fair to say that both 'O'Rang albums were as brilliant as they were flawed, but that's true of many of the greatest recordings.

Lee explained to *The Wire* magazine's Rob Young in 1996 that the name 'O' Rang stemmed from the lack of distinction drawn between man and ape in some Asian countries. In Asia, everything is 'Orang-something or other', he said.

The Slug studio in Tottenham, where *Herd Of Instinct* was recorded, was said to be kitted out like a primitive shrine complete with day-glow Aztec murals. The sensory weirdness of the *Spirit Of Eden* and *Laughing Stock* sessions would be ramped up for the *Herd Of Instinct* sessions, minus the austere restrictions Mark had imposed, replaced instead with a psychedelic party spirit and loads of guests popping in (and presumably, popping pills or other illicit substances) to participate on their own terms. It was said to be an exceptionally trippy experience at times, and that comes across on the album.

The basic template was that Paul and Lee would set the scene and jam endlessly, while friends would drop by and contribute if they were inspired to do so. These guests included guitarist Graham Sutton (whose own Bark Psychosis was hugely influenced by Talk Talk), Matt Johnson (whose group The The was one of the more singular acts of the '80s), Beth Gibbons (whose group Portishead released its classic trip-hop album *Dummy* the same year) and former Talk Talk regulars like Mark Feltham (harmonica), Martin Ditcham (percussion) and Simon Edwards (bass).

Engineer Phill Brown – who described the sessions as far more relaxed than those of *Laughing Stock* – was also coaxed back into the fold.

Nearly 30 years later, it's hard to think of an album that does what *Herd Of Instinct* does, to any great degree. Where the later Talk Talk albums (and especially Mark's album) were ascetic to the extreme, *Herd Of Instinct* tunes into something primal and pagan. For those willing to forge ahead through the thickets of jungle, there are deep grooves to be found. But it's also an album of sonic adventuring. Great delight is taken in the finding of odd tonalities and irruptive textures. At times it's feedback-drenched, so there's no mistaking this world music for the polite, clean, Euro-friendly world music-cum-disco of '90s dreck like Deep Forest.

While Lee and Paul take great delight in exploring their new multi-instrumentalism on the likes of didgeridoo, zurna, wood flute, harmonium, melodica and recorder, this is adventurism rather than colonialism at work, and at the heart of these musical rituals is a forgotten ancient Britain of pre-history. It's an astounding album, rich and rewarding, which sounds twice as nice late at night.

The album was received well by critics but sold only moderately. One reviewer wrote: 'Be thankful that albums with the depth and diversity of *Herd Of Instinct* can walk tall in a hostile environment. Inspired into a music which suggests, among other impossibilities, Van Morrison's *Astral Weeks* as recorded by Can in Kingston, Jamaica'.

Years later, Paul reminisced about the 'O' Rang experience:

We both dedicated three years experimenting with sound, performance and art behind galvanised steel doors at our base located in the heart of Tottenham Hale industrial estate. When entering this self-made environment, it seemed anything was possible and ideas could be explored and given space to thrive without being infected by outside influence. On reflection, it was a glorious time. A bridge crossing from our Talk Talk rhythm section days to an open-ended creative future. A future that I wouldn't have missed for the world. Lee and I adopted the attitude of creating music as if marooned on a desert Island, away from pre-fixed structure or outside influence, therefore recording music with no rules', he continued. 'A lot of these instruments we played in untutored ways, putting more emphasis on bringing out interesting characteristics from their sound, rather than learning to play them conventionally. In some ways, it was a child-like approach to making music, but with that mindset comes the intoxicating sense you have total freedom of expression.

Paul and Lee called the space The Slug because everything was allowed to evolve at a naturally slowed-down pace.

Herd Of Instinct's cover (and 24-page booklet) is a story in itself, and gives an indication of just how creatively oriented the 'O' Rang project was. Paul and Lee applied the same attitude to the artwork that they had to the music. Working with art director Cally Calloman, they built art installations in different locations to photograph, as well as creating oil paintings, collage, film, sculpture and mask making. Even the guest musicians got involved in the artwork. 'It was playful, enjoyable and all-consuming', said Paul.

The group never played any gigs. Long-deleted, *Herd Of Instinct* is being offered for a mere 700 pounds on Amazon. It has never been reissued, with rumours that the master tapes reside in a cupboard somewhere at BMG. Its music still defies description, and is like an intoxicating puzzle that can never quite be figured out or fully understood.

'Orang'

If you mean business, why not start with an epic? The 10 minutes and eight seconds of 'Orang' is not to be messed with, and it almost seems like it was intentionally placed right at the beginning to deter anyone who was there just to groove on down to 'Little Brother' or 'Mind On Pleasure'.

Dark and heady, the listener is immediately in a strange and morphing room, having a deep psychedelic experience.

There's a repeated descending riff that's performed with almost manic determination, a miscellany of feedback and other random sounds used to heighten the texture and tension, Lee doing his best Krautrock-style ritual drumming, and an indeterminate vocal that comes across like some Juju spirit chaser. Feltham's heavily processed diatonic harmonica is a key part of the texture of the piece.

The whole thing keeps moving and morphing like a hydra-headed snake, building and subsiding, heaving and releasing, potent as a magic spell from some ancient realm. Paul's voice occasionally doubles up with that of Beth Gibbons to speak in tongues. Towards the end, there's a spacey section worthy of Hawkwind in which Gibbons curls her voice into strange shapes. Hallucinogenic, to the max.

'Little Brother'

A slow, lumbering groove, half-submerged spoken words from what could be a tribal witch doctor. The percussion sounds part wooden, part metallic.

A female voice chants in an unknown language, and a stringent violin plays a musical sequence while flutes and other random elements fill up the sound field.

It's a very 'world' sound possibly geo-located in some primeval forest, a secret rite-cum-party, deep into the night. Feltham plays his most pungent harmonica on another piece that manages to fully justify its epic nine minutes and 27 seconds running time.

'Mind On Pleasure'

Another great stoned groove with a cool bassline and mad surging organ, 'Mind On Pleasure' is impossible not to want to shake your booty to, with its incredible loose-limbed drumming, elephantine horns and a female singing an alluring tantric line.

There's an exceptionally cool break-down with deep bass and drums that acknowledges the then hip drum and bass scene without simply aping it.

This is dance music but not as we know it: way too weird to have been acknowledged by any one of the prevailing trends that year, but nevertheless, it's a track that would get bums off seats and gyrating insanely on the dancefloor in the right circumstance.

In 1994 bands like The Happy Mondays and Primal Scream were welding rock music to dance grooves, trip-hop groups like Massive Attack were forging new sounds out of samples, there was the so-called acid-house scene cultivating an outlaw illegal rave culture, as well as the very hot drum and bass scene. Guest guitarist Graham Sutton would the very next year release his first drum and bass single under the name Boymerang, followed by an album of pulverising beats and textures in 1997. While 'O'Rang' were way to the left of centre and not part of any scene, they nevertheless explored the terrain around the edges of these musical scenes and the zeitgeist can be felt.

'All Change'

Signalling a short break from the intensity of the first three pieces, 'All Change' is simply a couple of minutes of jungle sounds with a spooky ecclesiastical inference, like the site of an old missionary station in the Amazon that's been reclaimed by the jungle and its inhabitants.

'Anaon, The Oasis'

'Take a mountain and smash it', announces a voice to trippy ambient drones and sound effects. Devoid of beats, the first part of the piece sounds like processed voices echoing through a cave, with an added thunderstorm and rain. It's really spooky.

Eventually, the slow beat of jungle drums, and an actual song of sorts appears, with Paul singing to a chorus of woodwinds, Jon Hassell-like horns and dissonant harmonica. He ends up in harmony with a female singer on a rather pretty kind of chant.

Paul wrote on his Facebook page that Matt Johnson of The The was integral to the creation of this track. 'Apart from being one of the most inventive songwriters of our generation, I can also vouch for his all-around gifted musicianship. When making the first 'O' Rang album, I invited Matt to join Lee Harris and I, for some free-flowing improvisation sessions. Although this was not something he was used to doing, Matt was effortlessly superb at it, resulting in the initial backbone of 'Anaon, The Oasis' being created between the three of us'.

'Loaded Values'
Paul's voice resembles a droll Thomas Dolby on 'Loaded Values', with its relentless percussion, vibraphone, wailing, distorted harmonica, chanted female chorus and busy atmosphere.

This is densely woven music that's packed with detail, as if escaping from Mark's equally intense minimalism. It feels very pagan with its rhythmic determination and wordless female ululations – a kind of dark trance music.

'Nahoojek-Foogoo'
This last track feels like a chance to wig out. There are drum machines, African xylophones, bongos and chants, as well as an overlay of spooky sonics.

The groove feels like it could go on forever, deep into the night, but after it gathers even more steam, the rhythms suddenly subside, allowing a cloud-covered industrial edifice to emerge from the deep jungle. Twisted sonics move through the spooky musical landscape and slowly fade away.

'O' Rang's one EP release, which preceded *Herd Of Instinct* in 1994, was built around a slightly different version of this track with a much shorter running time.

'O' Rang – Fields & Waves (1997)
Personnel:
Lee Harris: bass, drums, guitar, percussion, vocals, guitar, harmonica, Thai mouth organ, flute, sitar, Thai harp, clavinet, balalaika, didgeridoo, programming, editing.
Paul Webb: bass, vocals, guitar, accordion, Zin, Thai Mouth Organ, French horn, synth, Chinese violin, programming
Graeme Jones: guitar, sitar, bass, voice
Colette Meury: vocals
Simon Edwards: bass
Gena Dolganov: balalaika

Jaq Harris: vocal
Cally: floor sticks, eclectic generator
Graham Sutton: guitar
Beth Gibbons: voice
Produced by Lee Harris at The Slug.
Released 20 January 1997
UK release date: 20 January 1997
Running time: 68:00

No less dense or hallucinogenic, the second and, sadly, final 'O' Rang album necessitated a different approach to *Herd Of Instinct*, which was brought about by several practical matters. Firstly, during its gestation, they had to move out of the vast environs of The Slug studio warehouse and into a much smaller studio which couldn't accommodate the large number of guests. Secondly, according to Paul, a lot of their gear was starting to break down, which meant pauses in the schedule to carry out repairs. Paul says that the recorded album was lost twice due to malfunctioning gear, and in that sense was a bit of a nightmare.

The unintended upshot was that, without the long jam sessions to accommodate all the visiting musicians, the album – released in 1997 – became much more song-oriented, and Paul and Lee spent more time putting it together on their own. In fact, it represented the first real flowering of Paul's songwriting and featured substantially more of his vocals, and it's easy to hear this version of 'O' Rang in the twisted psychedelic pastoralism of Paul's later Rustin Man persona.

Working in a converted barn that was lined with harmoniums, the duo, as *The Wire* magazine noted at the time, 'had a playground of resonant materials: clapped out guitars played with beaters, a zither-like zin, sitars, Thai harps and mouth flutes, a Bali-phone, an old accordion'.

Much of the exoticism of *Herd Of Instinct* remained – or traces of it, in any case – but Phill Brown was absent, as was another important part of the original sound matrix, Mark Feltham. The heady party atmosphere of the debut was also missing, but it feels like Paul and Lee are getting closer to feeling confident enough to inch away from the more oppressive aspects of Talk Talk and move on to more personal projects.

There's a slight air of insubstantiality about the album as it progresses across its 68-minute running time, with some of its tracks sounding like little more than glorified grooves with psychedelic adornment. It's still a rich and rewarding record, but 13 tracks is a lot to digest and it's a less cohesive album as a whole than *Herd Of Instinct*.

It's doubtful that more than a small proportion of Talk Talk followers gave themselves fully to 'O'Rang – such is the deification of Mark – and it's likely that those who had checked out the first album and found it not to their taste won't have taken a chance on its sequel. Which is a pity. I get that to many of Mark's dedicated fans 'O'Rang would have been a step too far away from identifiable song structures, and that many of the vocals were impressionistic and seemed to glorify in their obscurity. But.

'O'Rang's meddling with exotic cultures could be seen as a kind of post-colonial meddling, as well, but really, that's one of the strengths of English culture: it comes from a conglomeration of different cultures and languages and has continued through popular music to absorb influences from primarily African-American culture while – in the case of Talk Talk and many others – somehow staying true to their inherent Englishness.

Paul and Lee were defiant in their intention to keep changing, and that 'O'Rang would never mean just one thing, stay in one place, or be just one sort of music. To that end, they talked about making 12-inch singles of 'dub and drum' music, but that wasn't to be. A third album, *Loudhailer No. 19*, was planned for 2001, but was never released.

'Barren'

The album begins with a wheezy harmonium followed by a relaxed, ambient groove featuring hammered dulcimer and other exotic instrumentation. It's rather gorgeous, with just enough of an edge to avoid comparisons with new age-leaning practitioners working in roughly the same zone.

Not only do we have an intriguing world music cocktail but one that applies itself with a psychedelic aesthetic by employing what appears to be the odd bit of sound manipulation, possibly captured during performance but more likely post-production jiggery-fuckery.

For instance, at one point, the music stops just long enough for a needle to skip across the grooves of a record (possibly influenced by the extensive use of this technique on The Mothers Of Invention's 1967 masterpiece, *We're Only In It For The Money*). After this brief moment in time, the groove starts up again and the hammered dulcimer is stereo-panned and then joined by celestial choral voices and a battery of percussion. The drums are noticeably crisper than on *Herd Of Instinct*.

It could also be claimed that glossy groups like Deep Forest are distant cousins of what 'O'Rang are doing here, but those fundamentally electronic bands don't have any of the deep atmosphere and mind-altering sounds that are prodigious on both *Herd Of Instinct* and *Fields And Waves*. Perhaps a closer cousin would be the ethno-medievalism of Dead Can Dance.

'Jalap'

The longest track on the album at 8:11, 'Jalap' finds Paul singing in a voice that's quintessentially English and of an age-old folk disposition. His is not a naturally gifted, soulful voice like Mark's, but is in the tradition of vocalists like Charles Hayward of This Heat, Richard Thompson and Matt Johnson – a voice that works well in context. You can imagine him in a pagan community a thousand years ago, telling strange and alluring folk tales to a gathering.

The instrumentation here includes pump organ, echoing voice, and subsidiary vocal lines sung by Beth Gibbons, as well as various found sounds and samples. Its lysergic qualities, together with the sensory overload of its various elements, makes it quite disorientating.

And like most of the songs on *Fields And Waves,* it has an almost Kraut-rock groove that keeps things ticking over nicely.

Note: Jalap is a medicinal plant that is used to cleanse the bowels. Was the name an attempt at humour, by any chance?

'P.53'

Beginning with metallic notes picked out on a Thai harp, 'No shame!' is the vocal refrain, and it's a phrase that gets repeated throughout the track. He's not credited, but I could swear Matt Johnson's voice can be heard on this track, although the main voice is Paul's.

Graeme Jones, a Wessex Sound Studios engineer, provides a squall of guitar, and the drum pattern is brisk and crisp, and goes at such a clip that it mirrors the drum and bass that was all the rage in 1996. There are spatial effects and breathy vocals.

'Moider'

This is a beatless soundscape with all the exotic elements we've come to expect from the group, including unhinged guitar, dulcimer and prodigious use of feedback. At just under five minutes, it doesn't outstay its welcome.

'Seizure'

There's a 'proper' vocal for a change which alternates between Paul and a mysterious female (Colette Meury). 'Seizure' has a groove of sorts. Graeme Jones handles the guitar.

'Moratorium'

Starting out as an ambient drone with a sensitive vocal by Paul, 'Moratorium' adds sitar and Asian chimes, which are eventually joined by a big drum and bass sound and a repeated vocal refrain of 'yeah-yeah-yeah-yeah'. There are large slabs of electric guitar as well.

'Superculture'

Jones switches from guitar to sitar for 'Superculture', which also features Thai mouth harp and, eventually, another crisp percussion pattern to keep it moving along. There's not much to this relatively short piece except that the various textures of its instrumentation make it a pleasurable listening experience.

'Quondam'

This is a nice stereo groove with big bass and echoed noises, which ends up sans drums and simply spacey sounds with double bass.

'Forest'

Featuring really fast drums, a rare appearance of orchestral keys, and harmonium. Occasionally, Paul's voice takes on the winsome quality of Robert Wyatt.

'Hoo'

With its pretty slide guitar, harmonium, almost-whispered voice, wooden flute and psychedelic spatial effects, 'Hoo' could almost be a lost Pink Floyd track from their immediate post-Syd Barrett period. The piece goes on for close to eight minutes with not much happening, but it goes nowhere very nicely indeed.

'Boreades'

There are strange noises, long bass notes, sonic irruptions and drawn-out keyboard notes. There's very definitely an 'end of record' mood on 'Boreades', which stops dead for some very wooden-sounding flute, balalaika and gentle percussion.

'Fields & Waves'

The title refers to quantum physics, as do the various artworks in the CD booklet. Starting with what sound like transmissions through space, the two minutes and four seconds of the title song then goes into an outro featuring what sounds like orchestral synth, and briefly back into orbital sound effects.

'Untitled'

This is a very short hidden track with jews harp.

Rustin Man

Beth Gibbons & Rustin Man – Out Of Season (2002)

Personnel:
Beth Gibbons: acoustic guitar, vocals
Rebecca Lublinski: flute
Rachael Samuel: cello
John Baggott: piano, Wurlitzer
Gary Baldwin: organ
John Barclay: flugelhorn
Martyn Baker: percussion, conga
Mark Berrow: violin
Rachael Brown: backing vocals
Ben Chappell: cello
Clive Deamer: drums
Philip Dukes: viola
Simon Edwards: bass
Mark Feltham: harmonica
Andrew Findon: flute
Pete Glenister: acoustic guitar
Leo Green: horn section
Lee Harris: drums
Nick Ingman: conductor, orchestration
Mitchell John: backing vocals
Patrick Kiernan: violin
Boguslaw Kustecki: violin
Peter Lale: viola
Martin Loveday: cello
Neill MacColl: acoustic guitar, e-bow
Perry Mason: violin
Lorraine McIntosh: backing vocals
Frank Ricotti: vibraphone
Eddie Roberts: violin
Nina Robertson: alto flute
Joy Rose: backing vocals
Mary Scully: double bass
Chris Tombling: violin
Jonathan Tunnell: cello
Adrian Utley: organ, guitar, bass, Moog synthesizer, e-bow
Bruce White: viola
Dave Woodcock: violin
Gavyn Wright: violin
Warren Zielinski: violin
Produced at The Barn, Sanctuary Westside Studios and Konk Studios by Beth
Gibbons and Paul Webb

UK release date: 28 October 2002
Highest chart places: UK: 28
Running time: 43:46

Paul Webb's 2002 collaboration with Beth Gibbons, on the face of it, seems unlikely. But it made perfect sense. In 1994, with partner Geoff Barrow, her project Portishead had released its wildly successful debut album, *Dummy*. The record's spooky combination of sampled cinematic strings and hip-hop beats combined with Beth's sultry vocals proved a sensation, and along with Tricky's *Maxinquaye* nudged the so-called 'trip-hop' genre into the mainstream.

Dummy came out the same year as 'O'Rang's *Herd Of Instinct,* on which Beth contributed some out-of-this-world vocal ululations. In effect, she was a member of the 'O'Rang collective, a friend of the family. In fact, she had auditioned as vocalist for 'O'Rang, but Portishead's unexpected success put paid to that idea.

By 2002, however, Portishead had become something of a burden. Beth, Geoff and third member Adrian Utley had moved on from the sound of *Dummy,* but the public and the press seemed unable to accept the group's rapid evolution. While Beth was seeking a creative outlet that wouldn't attract the same level of scrutiny or expectation, Paul had moved on from the communitarian philosophy of 'O'Rang as his writing skills had developed, and had come up with the Rustin Man nom de plume.

On *Out Of Season*, Paul's writing, arranging and production skills would be utilised by Beth, who was clearly looking for a way to combine her jazz diva influences with Paul's rustic English folk flavours. The combination of the two makes for an intriguing album, though the result is only partially successful. As a singer, Beth is almost the polar opposite to Mark Hollis. Where Mark is straight from the heart, pure soul and completely believable emotionally, Beth is somehow theatrical and showboaty. It's not that she's inauthentic, just that she's a stylist with a Billie Holiday affectation that can be hard to look past. Opinion is divided, however, and her success suggests that many get an emotional hit from her vocal presentation.

While the album was far from a chart-topper, it did do reasonably well, reaching 28 on the UK charts and number 6 in Norway. The same can't be said for the two 'O'Rang albums, which by 2002 had already sunk into obscurity.

Out Of Season was a chance for Paul to not only perform on multiple instruments, but also write and arrange, without the usual financial or organisational pressure. Recorded partially at Paul's home studio The Barn, but also at Sanctuary Westside and Konk Studios, the album featured an extensive supporting cast including a conductor of orchestration (Nick Ingman), Beth's Portishead collaborator Adrian Utley performing on a variety of instruments, and former Talk Talkers like Phill Brown, Lee Harris, Mark Feltham and Simon Edwards.

While *Out Of Season* is hardly a main course component for Talk Talk fans, it's a useful marker of Paul's development as a writer and producer, and an entrée to his later, more personal work under the Rustin Man banner. It's rather polite, however, and the big problem is that while Beth's tortured pity-me vocals worked brilliantly in the innovative context of the first Portishead album, they're not nearly as stand-out in this more conventional setup. *Mojo* magazine opined that it's 'among the best albums ever made', however, and *Uncut* put it at number 23 in their top 150 albums of the decade, so obviously, some pundits hold the album in very high esteem.

Note: The US edition features a 'bonus' song – a live rendition of Lou Reed's 'Candy Says'. The album was reissued in 2019 on vinyl.

'Mysteries' (Gibbons/Webb)
What's disappointing about *Out Of Season* is that the first sounds you hear are really alien, and you get all excited only to find that what follows is quite conventional, really. Beth's hushed and slightly anxious voice on 'Mysteries' is a lot like that of naïve hippy-folk singer Vashti Bunyan, however, and its exquisite arrangements (lovely acoustic guitar picking and old-fashioned, hymn-like choral backing) turn it into a rather haunting song. There's no connection to the *Twin Peaks* 'Mysteries Of Love' by Julee Cruise, but it's hard not to be charmed by its very English bucolic beauty.

'Tom The Model' (Gibbons/Webb)
'How can I forget your tender smile/Moments I have shared with you?' The lyrics might be a little hackneyed, but 'Tom The Model' is intentionally very old-fashioned – especially in the chorus, when it goes into a 1960s soul sound with horns and organ. There are also strings and backing singers in evidence.

'Show' (Gibbons)
Beth gets to act out the diva on this self-written piece with just lonely piano, cello and flute accompaniment. She comes on like a wasted Billie Holiday-type jazz singer.

'Romance' (Gibbons/Webb)
There are creamy strings and mellow horns in this low-key number.

'Sand River' (Webb)
Most compositions are collaborations between Beth and Paul (presumably Beth's lyrics and Paul's music), but here, Paul gets a lone writing credit, and it's possibly the best song on the album. Instrumentation includes acoustic guitar, acoustic bass, smooth backing vocals and Theremin.

'Spider Monkey' (Gibbons/Webb)
This is a hushed kind of folk music with a bit of mystery in its bones. 'Time is but a memory', Beth sings. There are guitars, an electric piano, and it ends with a cute-sounding mechanical instrument.

'Resolve' (Gibbons/Webb)
Beth's voice drops a notch for this love-lost song featuring lone acoustic guitar.

'Drake' (Gibbons/Webb)
'I don't know why you had to go', she sings, to a lonely harmonica solo. There's also acoustic guitar and bass, and a shaker.

'Funny Time Of Year' (Gibbons/Webb)
There's a slightly spaghetti western feel to 'Funny Time Of The Year, with its shimmering electric guitar. Occasionally she's almost Nick Cave-like in her existential darkness.

'Rustin Man' (Gibbons/Webb)
Clearly, the song from which Paul took the name for his project henceforth, Beth uses her Portishead voice for a piece that feels largely improvised.

Rustin Man – Drift Code (2019)
Personnel:
Paul Webb: vocals, piano, electric guitar, guitarron, electric bass, organ, synthesizer, baritone guitar, electric piano, acoustic guitar, xylophone, 12-string guitar, accordion, harmonica
Lee Harris: drums, sitar, Jaw's harp, tambourine
TJ Mackenzie: euphonium, trumpet, trombone, flugelhorn, French horn
Snowboy: claviola, surdo, pandeiro, rattle, chimes
Catherine Chandler: violin, viola, viola d'amore
Ginny Davis: cello
Nancy Lewis: flute
James Yorkston: clarinet
Stephanie Hedges: vocals
Sam Webb: vocals
Grace Webb: backing vocals
Produced at Barnlight Studios by Rustin Man/Paul Webb.
UK release date: 1 February 2019
Running time: 38:04

Drift Code must have had not only the longest gestation of any album connected to the members of Talk Talk, but of just about any album by anyone, ever. Paul started recording in 2004, but the album wasn't completed until 2018 (it was released the following year). That's 14 long years, and 18 since the release of *Out Of Season*, his collaboration with Beth Gibbons.

It's not clear exactly why the album took so long, but he did have to take breaks to produce a few albums for other bands and artists, most notably James Yorkston in 2006, Swedish group The Tiny in 2008, and Belgian group Dez Mona in 2009. But Paul has talked about how he wanted to play most of the instruments, and that to do so, he had to learn how to play them all to the standard he required. In the end, musicians were brought in to add strings and horns, but Paul's performances form the backbone of the recordings.

Some insight into the process, however, can be gleaned from an interview with *Prog* magazine's Joe Banks, in which he described the relaxed painterly process he used. Each of the tracks started with bass and drums and over time – sometimes years – he would add more instruments. This methodology meant that there were many songs in various stages of completion. Paul describes how, at a certain point, a particular instrument would cease to feel like something he'd performed and would simply belong to that song.

Although Paul had used his voice occasionally in 'O'Rang, *Drift Code* marks the first time that he's officially tasked with being the singer, and he carries it off with aplomb. His approach to singing, and indeed to his music in general, is completely oblivious to trend, connecting instead with what the song requires. Paul's singing and overall music style have been compared to great English eccentrics like Robert Wyatt and Syd Barrett, but really, the great connection between them is that there is no connection: there's certainly a similar sense of Englishness, but beyond that, the similarity is that each one of them is so completely themself. Tonally, there is sometimes a slight resemblance to both Peter Hammill of Van Der Graaf Generator and David Bowie, and the way he sometimes stretches his vocal cords past what is comfortable is reminiscent of Blue Nile's Paul Buchanan.

Rustin Man might at first seem rather toned down compared to the halcyon days of Talk Talk and 'O'Rang, and any experimentation is tied to actual songs, with more orthodox structures and real choruses. But *Drift Code*'s footprint isn't quite like anything else. Long gone is the time when Paul's wiggly fretless bass was his most recognisable contribution, and each song is a veritable world unto itself, endlessly inventive and thought-through.

A big part of this unique musical aesthetic clearly originates from where it's recorded, at his home in Essex, which doubles as a recording studio. As Paul notes on the Rustin Man website: 'I've come to believe that the space in which you write or record music is extremely important and that it's worth making this environment as magical and unique as you possibly can; the theory being that the magic and uniqueness affect the way you're working and seep into the music somehow. For me, a studio should feel like a playground, with an atmosphere that frees the spirit and allows you to go wherever your imagination leads you'.

Paul goes on to detail how The Barn was a vast empty shell on a field when he bought it, but that over the years, they've added 'statues, ornaments and other oddities to intermingle with musical instruments and hidden microphone cables. The Hammond organ doubles up as a clothes shelf and the sleeping harmonium proudly displays memorabilia on top of it. There are golden velvet draped curtains and a large number of fairy lights dangling from the ceiling. Collectively, all these things have turned the barn into our own little world, a remote island of treasures that time has forgotten, gently influencing our lives and the music on a subconscious level'.

Mojo magazine made *Drift Code* their album of the month, and it was generally critically acclaimed without making a dent on the mainstream music market.

'Vanishing Heart'
Paul has said that Rustin Man lyrics are not necessarily from personal experience, but more likely characters created to tell stories. On 'Vanishing Heart', he's escaped the clutches of someone who lied and caused him pain, and is now in a much stronger position; one in which he can laugh at and even mock this person.

His vocals are austere, and the mournful chorus is like a kind of blues chant. The song is populated by guitar and piano, organ and jangly guitar.

'Judgement Train'
There's a train whistle, the sound of steam and a boarding announcement before this old-time blues/gospel number gets rolling. It's the kind of song you can almost imagine Tom Waits writing.

The character thinks he can actually dupe God. 'I pulled a card from lucky hat/See I'm always good at rigging games... So now Lord, I'm number one/ Let me raise the pearly gates'. Except, of course, that it's not that simple.

The song features wah-wah guitar and interestingly, dual guitar and flute lines.

'Brings Me Joy'
On the face of it, a song about the sheer enjoyment of 'hearing angels sing', 'Brings Me Joy' features fruity church organ, a lovely soprano voice, and Paul sounding as close as he ever got to a fusion of Robert Wyatt and Peter Hammill.

'Our Tomorrows'
Seemingly a song about the impossibility of completely living in the moment, and freezing a moment of bliss between two people, life always moving on.

'Our Tomorrows' is oddly reminiscent of The Doors' classic 'LA Woman' with its dominant electric piano. There are definitely hallucinogens in this musical mixture, along with a memorable chorus, beautiful vocal harmonies (presumably Paul overdubbing himself) and, at the end, a powerful big band!

'Euphonium Dream'

The only instrumental on *Drift Code,* the title is apt as there are indeed euphoniums and other horns, but also a strange, organ-like sounds and other processed instruments. Very odd but rather intoxicating.

'The World's In Town'

Possibly a song about the separation of death through a cosmic perspective, the narrator notes that 'I'm floating across the sea/The world is a feeling in song!' and 'I'm part of the milky way/I'm drifting day to day'. Home, and a town, isn't enough. He's stardust.

Paul's vocals are Bowie-ish on this big ballad, and there's even what appears to be a choir.

'Light The Light'

Musically, 'Light The Light' is the strangest track on *Drift Code.* It begins with a playful piano line, then bursts into life with a circus organ, some wah-wah guitar and a very odd vocal. Darkly humorous and quite bizarre, it's a song that appears to implore everyone to follow their passions, be themselves, and not to go quietly into the night.

'Martian Garden'

Featuring one of the wordiest lyrics of any Rustin Man song, the meaning eludes this writer, but perhaps Paul is talking about moving on from those things that are not important in life, not getting caught up in meaningless or irrelevant distractions: 'I'm closing down/The whole fairground'.

Musically, it's full of the kind of imaginative lysergic motifs and textures that made the work of late '60s and early '70s songwriters like Kevin Ayers so rich and absorbing. If anyone claims that Paul isn't still making courageous or unique music in his post 'O'Rang guise, play them this!

'All Summer'

This gorgeous, passionate ballad, sans drums and featuring mainly acoustic guitar and piano, contains some surprising instrumental lines – the sort of imaginative insertions and ideas that can only eventuate from tinkering, rather than a band playing in a room together.

Again, only Paul really knows what the lyrics allude to, but they feel a lot like the way an understanding parent might respond to a teenager who is throwing around hurtful comments as she strains to leave the nest: 'It's alright to say you hate me/Tire me out and call me dated/You've been caught in the crossfire/Growing up in the grass/All summer'.

Rustin Man – Clockdust (2020)

Personnel:
Paul Webb: vocals, piano, acoustic guitar, electric bass, guitarron, backing

vocals, electric guitar, baritone guitar, electric piano, organ, ukulele, synthesizer, dulcimer, harmonica, xylophone, effects, melodica, handclaps, washboard, tambourine, claves
Lee Harris: drums, handclaps
Snowboy: congas, bongos, percussion, pandeiro, temple block, cowbell, tambourine, bullroarer, timbales, rattle, guiro, rainstick, shaker, chimes, claviola
Catherine Chandler: violin, viola
TJ Mackenzie: flugelhorn, French horn, trumpet, euphonium, trombone
Catherine Begley: backing vocals
Stephanie Hedges: backing vocals
Sam Webb: backing vocals, handclaps
Ginny Davis, cello
Produced at Barnlight Studios by Rustin Man/Paul Webb.
UK release date: 20 March 2020.
Running time: 39:46

Released on the day the UK went into its first Covid-19 lockdown in 2020, *Clockdust* is a companion piece to *Drift Code*. Its songs were recorded concurrently and tinkered with for many years. Nevertheless, the variety of available material meant that in the song selection process, Paul was able to create two distinct albums with different moods and musical aspects.

The big difference is that *Clockdust* is more acoustically oriented, although it does deviate from that occasionally. Because it's sparer and moodier than its predecessor, his vocals are more to the fore. Sometimes, when he reaches for a note, it's a bit of a stretch and a squeeze. That might annoy some and won't bother others. In any case, it's not as worrying as Blue Nile's Paul Buchanan, and no one seemed to mind his insistent over-reaching.

He had been planning a series of concerts for the first time in many years, but the Covid pandemic put paid to that. Nevertheless, the album garnered many effusive reviews, *The Guardian* writing that it sports 'ageless and eerily beautiful compositions'.

'Carousel Days'
Another song of regret, 'Carousel Days' holds up a period of time as representative of freedom and the height of fun, and everything since a diminishment.

The piano notes are gently depressed; the guitar is gently reverbed, the female backing is gently sung, the brass is gently parped.

'Gold & Tinsel'
Is 'Gold & Tinsel' about the insatiable demand from the music industry for more, more, more music even when it's not up to scratch? And looking, always looking for the next hot thing? Who knows, but its lyrics are intriguing, with lines like: 'Look how they want more/Whenever the

rhyming comes/There's a dusty old bandstand/Full of new guitars/Waiting to misbehave'.

It's another gorgeous ballad with acoustic guitar, a cute 'organ' sound, strings, and female backing vocals.

'Jackie's Room'

'She's a book you won't get through', Paul sings about the object of his obsession. He can't get enough of her, etcetera.

There's a fabulous call-and-response section (a chorus of Pauls responding to Paul, that is) in this atmospheric song.

'Love Turns Her On'

Dramatic, turbulent and with some dissonant, angry-sounding guitar at the climax, it's not surprising to learn that 'Love Turns Her On' is about jealousy.

'Rubicon Song'

As with *Drift Code,* there's an instrumental slap bang in the middle, and this is it. And once again, while it's something of a break from the programme, it's also one of the highlights. In fact, it's so strange that it could pass for intermission music at the movies on some alien planet, as depicted in a sci-fi show from the 1950s. There are weird, looped voices, xylophones, and goodness knows what else.

'Old Flamingo'

Paul has spoken about his wide-ranging influences throughout recorded music history, and 'Old Flamingo', though it's clearly a creation of the 21st century, takes and generously flouts its love of 1940s smooch. It's never less than ambitious in its nostalgia. There's a brass band and reverbed guitars and Paul's voice is at a softer, higher pitch. Meanwhile, the words tell a story about a woman who has escaped the clutches of someone unworthy – a song of encouragement and moving on.

'Kinky Living'

This story-song about 'a discrete woman/selling herself down the river' is very Tom Waits, from its rundown circus rhythms to its mix of xylophones and horns. Heck, even the guitar solo sounds like something from *Swordfishtrombones*. But hey, that's no bad thing!

'Night In Evening City'

Somewhat out of character with the acoustically oriented *Clockdust,* 'Night In Evening City' is easily the longest song at 7:18 and the piece most concerned with its sonics.

With its patter of bongos, astringent Hollis-like guitar, harmony background singing and the unlikeliest of solos (via the Clavioline and xylophone, respectively), the song is full of strange effects and ultimately, Paul gets out his bass for a dub outro. I'm sure we can all live with that!

'Man With A Remedy'

In essence, 'Man With A Remedy' is Paul's own take on a subject first raised by Frank Zappa in his 1974 song, 'Cosmik Debris'. While that song was a coruscating attack on those figures who always seem to hang out to exploit musicians – drug dealers, magic potion makers, 'problem solvers' of all kinds – Paul's song focuses more on the state of the musicians themselves: 'So if he's a man with a remedy, he's catching us all unaware/And if he's the man with a remedy/Then we've gone too far to really care'.

The song itself is about as pop-oriented as *Clockdust* gets and sounds like a full band that, in someone's fevered imagination, could have been a contemporary of psychedelic-era Beatles. Except that, as the piece progresses, it evolves from psych to psychotic. Clever.

Tim Friese-Greene

Of all the former Talk Talk associates, Tim Friese-Greene is the hardest to get a handle on. A musician/producer who ended up becoming Mark's closest writer/collaborator and an essential component on the best of the group's musical output, bizarrely, he was never an official Talk Talk member.

While the main impetus and vision of Talk Talk may have been Mark, it's likely that without Tim's particular skills, the group would never have found its feet. Try picturing *The Colour Of Spring, Spirit Of Eden* and *Laughing Stock* without Tim: it just does not compute.

It's unclear how the two personalities played off each other, but obviously, the creative relationship between Mark and Tim worked well, and for that to continue for as long as it did, there had to be both understanding and respect flowing between them.

It's clear from Tim's post-Talk Talk music projects that in Talk Talk, Tim wasn't simply a 'make it happen' guy for Mark but a true collaborator with his own ideas and a steely resolve to do it his way. Having said that, Talk Talk was primarily Mark's baby, so it's likely that part of Tim's work was practical, working as an enabler for Mark's sometimes fanciful ideas.

At the end of *Laughing Stock,* Tim was ready to walk. Pragmatic to the end, he knew that the creative relationship had run its course and that he needed to move on. From then on, he would tend to pick and choose his production jobs, working as both producer and player with bands and artists that he liked. Jobs he would take on included Lush and Catherine Wheel. But eventually, he stopped accepting production commissions to concentrate on his own work. And he knew that he had to find his own way.

'When I first came back to writing and performing', he said, 'having finished with production, my main goal was to avoid sounding like the band that I'd just spent ten years working with. It was the opposite of copying something – I was trying to forget something'.

In 1997, Tim released the first EP by his Heligoland project. Unlike Mark, he had the skills to be almost completely self-contained, and unlike Paul, he found himself rebelling at the idea of collaborating with others, becoming something of a DIY one-man band.

The rich irony was that Tim had been involved in some of the most skilfully performed, carefully engineered and brilliantly produced recordings of the '80s and '90s, but that he made a conscious aesthetic decision to throw that away with his own work. Having rejected the high-gloss audiophile sound of *The Colour Of Spring* and helped to launch the lo-fi post-rock genre with *Laughing Stock,* he now saw a completely different way of working.

'People don't like the idea of their records sounding worse than their demos', Tim says. 'For me, people's demos are almost invariably better sounding than their final records. I don't mean better in terms of their fidelity. I mean better in terms of how interesting, how charismatic, how endearing, how moving they are. Musicians doing demos are more likely to do things off the top of their heads, because they are doing things as the inspiration strikes them rather than copying something and trying to improve on it further down the line when they feel that they have got to accommodate the record company or their listening public. A lack of finesse is really important to me because all it signifies to me is a lack of production, a lack of a barrier between the playing and the listening. I now see production in that respect as being a largely negative thing'.

If anything, the slim discography released under the Heligoland banner is the imperfect exposition of that philosophy. These are raw, often intentionally distorted recordings that Tim has worked up with little outside input, as he feels no need to collaborate with others, enjoying feeding off his own creativity without the burden of having to discuss ideas.

Outside of Heligoland, Tim has released several idiosyncratic albums under his own name and one, Short-haired Domestic, with his partner.

If there's a problem with Tim's post-Talk Talk creative endeavours, it's that his single-mindedness can sometimes feel too insular and feel like it could benefit from the contributions of others. There's a bloody-mindedness to his work that betrays an almost punk-like attitude. That's refreshing, and it's gratifying that his creative path defies the music industry by refusing to participate in any conventional career development. But at the same time, this attitude helps to explain Tim's surprisingly low profile.

Beware: If you search for Heligoland on music streaming services, make sure you're not listening to the putrid and hugely boring work of the France-based Australian outfit who go by the same name, or the Massive Attack album called *Heligoland*. Tim's Heligoland is available exclusively through Bandcamp.

Heligoland – Creosote & Tar EP (1997)

Personnel: Tim Friese-Greene
Produced in the attic of a house in South London by Tim Friese-Greene
UK release date: 1 January 1997
Running time: 17:40

Like every subsequent recording, Heligoland's debut EP was released on Tim's own label, Calcium Chloride. Released in the wake of 'O'Rang's second album, *Fields & Waves,* and the year before Mark Hollis's own album, the differences are telling. While Lee and Paul in 'O'Rang sounded like they relished their freedom from Mark's iron grip on every tiny part of the process, they still sounded as though there were elements of the Talk Talk sound that they wanted to further expound upon. Tim, in contrast, sounded on his Heligoland project as though he wanted to move as far away from the Talk Talk template as possible to discover his own muse. And while Mark, on his last album, sounded in retreat from the world, Heligoland from the get-go, sounded vital, engaged, in-the-moment and engorged with lo-fi, DIY spirit.

Originally worked up 'on Osea island in the Blackwater estuary', the sound had one thing in common with *Laughing Stock*: the lo-fi approach and appreciation of 'non-musical' elements like hum, feedback and random interference.

The EP and Tim's Heligoland project in general, also show a man newly infatuated with electric guitar. While his performative duties in Talk Talk were mostly on various keyboards, *Creosote & Tar* and the two Heligoland albums would delight in the noise-making thrill of electric guitar. This may well have continued had Tim not increasingly suffered from tinnitus.

'Creosote & Tar'

The first track on the first Heligoland EP is like all the discord on *Laughing Stock* amplified, and it's relentless in its pursuit of its quite nasty punk sound. There's grungy guitar, overloaded sonics, half-buried instruments (is that harmonica deep in the mix?), cool riffing, and Tim's vocals work well as a kind of cross-current against the repetitive guitar figure.

'Dreaming Of Persephone'

'Dreaming Of Persephone' starts with a raw, rude guitar playing a rather odd, wonky repeated figure, and Tim's voice sounds like a low-rent cross between Mark and Jeff Buckley. Eventually, there's a rudimentary, relentlessly banging drum. 'Shield my eyes from your gamine dress/Save my hand from your milky skin', he sings. His lyrics sound smart, but it's impossible to hear enough of them through the noise.

'Blued'

'Blued' starts with some kind of found sound (rain on gravel?) a very raw-sounding drumkit and angry guitar, then a really rude, shrieking Variophon solo (or some other novelty keyboard). Almost punk, it's so contrary, like he's blowing a raspberry at expectations. Later, there's a cheap organ sound. At 6:29, 'Blued' has time to stretch its legs. Some mellow piano, buried in the mix until now, appears in stark contrast at the end and the beat goes on and on, until it stops.

'The Kiss-Off'

Tim's crooned vocal is a nice contrast to the exceptionally gnarly guitar and general roughness of 'The Kiss Off'.

Heligoland – Heligoland (2000)

Personnel:
Tim Friese-Greene: vocals, instruments and samplers
Jim White: drums
Dominic Kelly: oboe
Mick Foster: saxophone

Robert Spriggs: viola
Lee Howton: voice
Tim Shepard: noises
Rob and Neil: percussion
Produced by Tim Friese-Greene
Released: 1 January 2000
Running time: 40:00

The debut Heligoland album comes nearly three years after the first EP and it's much more accomplished but is still soaked in plenty of cool guitar riffing and relishes in the noise an electric guitar can make.

It's still determinedly lo-fi and that has both pros and cons. While Tim's ideas are never diluted and there's excitement in hearing the spark of creation without mediation or second sight, sometimes I find myself yearning for the kind of instrumental variation that comes from collaboration.

For instance, Tim often favours a monotonous drum machine beat which seems counter-intuitive. There's a lot to like, however, despite his monomaniacal pursuits.

'Lost & Lethal'
The first thing you notice is how much more confident Tim's singing is. He's no Mark Hollis, but he can wrap his voice around a tune, and express himself vocally. 'Throw me a line and wish me well', he sings to a very insistent circular riff while the maelstrom slowly builds.

'Shrug'
'If there's no time to love you now/There's no time to cry', he sings with a close-miked voice to a strummed acoustic guitar and swishing drum machine. Tim brings out one of those funny wee keyboards for a faux-orchestral effect. There's an almost folk tinge to 'Shrug'.

'Bluebird'
Tim's guitar riffing is one of the real highlights as he brandishes his instrument in a manner familiar to fans of groups like Sonic Youth or, more accurately, Bailter Space. On 'Bluebird', he doggedly pursues just a few elements for its 6:26 running time, multi-tracking guitar, drum machine, random cheap keyboards, with a nasty climax that sounds like a broken down Mellotron. 'You talk in tongues/You bend the air/You say the revolution starts here', he sings.

'Relapse'
This is a short interlude with wind instruments. 'Mosquito/How you plague me/Take your sickly whine away/I am so tired of this noise'.

'Shock Treatment'
Heavy guitar chording with an undertow of clarinet, 'Shock Treatment' is one of the darker tracks with its dynamic contrasts, bursts of noise and, at one point, a strange voice repeating something indeterminate over and over. Cool riffs, again!

'Isn't It Sad'
Once again, Tim uses soft/loud dynamics effectively on 'Isn't It Sad', with some angry guitar riffing towards the end and his 5-string guitar bending the notes deliciously. I like the mid-section, in which clarinets parp like geese in heat.

'Loaded Gun'
On this more relaxed, low-key song, Tim's voice is more audible, and he has an almost Bob Dylan inflection – that breathy, 'constipated wheeze' familiar to fans of the folk-rock bard. The loping beat and friendly organ make a nice change, and there's even a whistling section!

'Sick Baby You'
Tim sounds a lot like John Lennon when he sings the title of this brief piece, which seems to be about some crazy former love interest.

'The Kiss-Off'
Tim's vocal is a bit buried on this last track, but the nasty guitar sonics and cheap-sounding organ that feature prominently on the album are back, and there's an effective dynamic.

Heligoland – Pitcher, Flask & Foxy Moxie (2006)
Personnel:
Tim Friese-Greene: vocals, instruments and samplers
Mikey Kirkpatrick: flute
Naomi Allnut: violin
Sarah Humphreys: shawm
Lee Friese-Greene: backing vocals
Tracey Howton: backing vocals
Produced in a disused mattress factory in Devon by Tim Friese-Greene
Released: 1 January 2006
Running time: 43:22

Described by Tim as 'still much a guitar record' despite the increasing sophistication of his second album as Heligoland, the name *Pitcher, Flask & Foxy Moxie* 'signifies the polarisation of recording techniques', says Tim. 'The very low end is represented by a pitcher or a flask. They are earthenware vessels and, therefore, very primitive. That represents the most basic sort of recording technique that I use. Moxie, in contrast, is a computer recording language, so that represents the kind of digital age if you like. It is a symbol to me of the fact that the album uses very low ends of technology and then very high ends of technology at the same time'.

Disaster struck when Tim's hard drive died just before he was going to back up a whole summer's work. 'I lost about thirty overdubs, which was one of the most distressing things that has ever happened to me in my life. I had to go back and redo all this stuff that I was really happy with. The album never recovered from that in my eyes. I never felt the same about it. Once I had lost all that stuff, it was only ever going to be a second best for me. Nobody else would spot it, but for me, it was really all spoiled. It was never going to be the same again. Until then, it was shaping up to be an album that I would actually really like'.

It would end up being the last guitar-based, raw-sounding Heligoland recording and, to date, the last Heligoland album.

'Wedding Feast'
Somewhat hampered by an annoying drum machine sound, 'Wedding Feast' is typical of the rest of the album: Tim's voice has gained again in confidence and ability, and the song itself is a kind of psychedelic power pop with a bit of dirty guitar, piano and one of those cheap-sounding keyboards he loves so much. The wordplay is playful and witty throughout.

'Semantics Got Me Caned'
Where previous Heligoland tracks kept fairly religiously to a kind of lo-fi rock template, suddenly, he opens things up to sneaky grooves that verge on swing blues. There's a memorable chorus featuring female backing singers, where he sings: 'You'll be on the rack' to their answer of 'No-no-no-no!' and a rather humorous-sounding keyboard solo. Tim's playful croon reminds me of Bid from the always-entertaining Monochrome Set.

'Black Girl'
A really dirty-sounding piece that grinds along on one chord. There's piano here, buried way down in the bowels of the mix.

'Fruit'
More dirt: dirty guitar, dirty harmonica, more grinding away. At 3:12, there's a child's voice, after which Tim begs: 'People, people, won't you help her out for me?' And he's suddenly a sensitive troubadour singing to a lone acoustic guitar and flute!

'The War, Stupid'
Tim's been quoted as saying that he's not interested in politics and issue-based songs, but 'The War, Stupid' certainly sounds like he has something to say, even if my ears can't hear the precise run of lyrics over the over-amped guitar noise. And it sounds serious, like he really means it. Even the

chord progression is serious. And he takes a few solos (guitar, keyboard) that are pure angry/sonic expression, taking a few leaves from Talk Talk's late-period book.

'Clasp'
'You're still my little girl', he sings on 'Clasp', a groove of sorts that eventually cuts back to just guitar, drums and voice.

'Down To Zero'
No wonder Tim got tinnitus with all this guitar squall. It's loud and he wrenches some between-note riff damage out of his 5-string guitar before a female singer throws a few lines our way and the guitar returns for some wah-wah action.

'3 Stills'
On '3 Stills', I can't help but wish for more sonic variation. The drum machine is so monochromatically repetitive; the mix is muddy and ... next!

'She Walked With Me To The End Of The Stars'
The last track and a long one at 7:10. This one sports a folk-like melody along with a bit of female voice and melodic violin. It's a ballad with piano and one of Tim's odd keyboards tootling away, the only annoyance being that damn drum machine.

Heligoland – One Girl Among Many EP (2014)
Personnel:
Tim Friese-Green: all instruments
Steve Dayment: trumpet
Jack Ross: Turkish drum
Lee Friese-Greene: backing vocals
Gretchen Faust: backing vocals
Kathy Welch: backing vocals
Produced by Tim Friese-Green
Released: 1 January 2014
Running time: 17:58

'This EP represents all I managed to complete of an album of mainly Latin-inflected Hammond organ songs before being laid low with hearing problems', wrote Tim on his website.

While *Pitcher, Flask & Foxy Moxie* suggested an imminent move away from the gritty lo-fi guitar sonics that had defined Heligoland since 1997, *One Girl Among Many* represented a complete move away from rock.

Tim makes the point that the vinyl mixes are intentionally mellower than the digital ones, which are 'a bit grittier as well'.

'One Girl Among Many'
The title track is very different from everything that came before: a squidgy synth figure over which samples of various political commentary are played, before he starts singing in a significantly deeper voice. The big shock, however, is that he employs a house beat, though I don't really see anyone dancing to this.

'Song With No Refrain'
'Song With No Refrain' has a delightfully distorted bass, organ, and a vocal style that's quite up-close and intimate in a Matt Johnson mode, with a bit of croon. Oh, and female backing singers going 'la-la-la-la-la'. It's crazy and unpredictable.

'A Bust Flush From A To Z'
'I don't know why a random bunch of notes can make you cry... I don't know how love's so profound', croons Tim to this slinky tune with female backing singers and trumpet.

'Such Is My Dismay'
Boasting fruity organ, jingling drums and once again, newly minted deeper crooning vocals, 'Such Is My Dismay' seemingly bears no relation at all to previous Heligoland releases.

Tim Friese-Greene – 10 Sketches For Piano Trio (2009)
Personnel:
Tim Friese-Greene: all instruments
Produced by Tim Friese-Green at The Hold, Totnes
Released: 1 January 2009
Running time: 24:00

The 'piano trio' in this case is Tim, Tim and Tim. The idea was to explore the nature of improvisation by constructing these ten sketches as if the piano, bass and drums were actually intuiting in real-time. It's an odd idea and the reality of it is not quite here nor there.

The intention was never to attempt to play jazz, just to use a line-up that's typically employed by jazz musicians. In fact, the jazz trio has such a long heritage that it's almost impossible to think of it any other way: the mere sound of piano, acoustic bass and drums together instantly denotes jazz in our minds, whether it's genuinely improvisational or not.

In actuality, Tim's music has never made more than a passing glance at jazz, and as he recorded/overdubbed the piano, bass and drums separately, while there are improvised elements, it's a construction and an intentional fabrication.

As Tim comments on his website:

In truth, this was the first time I'd ever seriously picked up a pair of drum sticks, and was keen to avoid any looping or playing to clicks. I think this

123

gives it a genuine, singular, and very necessary punk edge – it was never my intention to make some kind of proper jazz record; that would've been just too crass.

The idea has legs, but can a punk-influenced writer/producer really make something new with such well-worn elements? Predictably, Tim's novice drumming means that the thing doesn't swing like jazz, and the bass playing also sounds fraudulent. Is it even acoustic bass? While he's a capable pianist, he certainly lacks the light and infinitely subtle touch of the best acoustic jazz pianists.

There's just too much history behind the piano trio line-up to write a new chapter, and these sketches inevitably end up sounding just a little square, if not clunky. And while there are vague changes of tone or mood over its nine tracks, there's an overall sameness that makes them all blend together.

Consequently, I've not reviewed the individual tracks, which don't have titles but are simply listed from 1 to 10.

Tim Friese-Greene – Melodic Apoptosis (2022)

Personnel:
Tim Friese-Greene: melodica, drums, string section
Produced by Tim Friese-Green in the roof of a deserted language school
Released: 22 July 2022
Running time: 24:00
Tracklisting: 'She Didn't Look Back', '...Les Voiles Tournent Encore!', 'Wreckage Slow To Surface', 'Wraiths On The Beach At Dawn', 'What Can Be Saved', 'Beset By Thinking Plague', 'Homeostasis Of The She-Light', 'Homeostasis Of Acceptance'

This surprise eight-track mini-album under Tim's own name, which was recorded during the first Covid-19 lockdown in 2020, combines vibraphone, keyboard, strings and drums. By dint of its instrumental line-up, the album is immediately reminiscent of easy listening 'exotica' records from the late 1950s and early 1960s when LPs were still quite new to market and stereo and 'hi-fi' was a brand-new phenomenon.

Tim's compositions don't have the lilt of those old exotica records, though. Instead, each of these tracks sounds like it could be a try-out for a film soundtrack. Most of the album is fairly easy on the ear and pleasant because of the inherent schmaltziness of the instruments.

There are no vocals, but the album is reminiscent of Heligoland in one way: the instrumentation and approach is the same throughout. There is little variety aside from the slightly different moods from song to song. I'd love to report that *Melodic Apoptosis* reveals a bold new direction for Tim and his music, but apart from the unusual instrumentation, it's more of the same-same-same all the way through.

What next? Gamelan on the moon?

Short-haired Domestic – Short-haired Domestic (2020)

Personnel:
Tim Friese-Green: instruments
Lee Friese-Greene: vocals, instruments
Produced by Tim Friese-Green at The Hold, Totnes
Released: 5 June 2020
Running time: 46:23

The rough edges and gnarly guitars were long gone by the time this project with Tim's wife, Lee Friese-Greene, hit digital outlets in 2020. It's a rather eccentric and undeniably fun-filled album, the idea of which is based around nine songs, each sung in a different language.

'I realized that Lee had a talent for picking up the nuances of other languages, and that got me thinking how that could best be utilised', said Tim.

'Musically, the concept was Tim's – to write an album with each song in a different language, exploring the idea of how much of the meaning and feel of a song can be conveyed musically', said Lee.

'Musically, I was on my own', said Tim, 'which is the only way I can really work, as I am so used to making hundreds of decisions a day... 99 per cent without consciously thinking about them at all, or even having to acknowledge them as questions. I would find it really laborious to have to externalise these, and can't imagine how I ever did it'.

Tim used mostly 1990s breakbeat loops, with some tracks accentuating bass, or synth, or guitar. '[It was] pretty much in a style you could generically call funk', said Tim, 'and synths would be kind of dark and squelchy or discordant'.

As any fan of world music knows, it often doesn't matter that you can't understand the language because you still get the feeling from the sound of the voice. And as eccentric as this project would seem, it's both intriguing and fun to listen to. Native speakers of the various languages might be able to pick out mispronunciations, but to my ears, Lee's singing sounds effortless and natural.

Some will view this as an indulgence, but if you forget about the conceptual conceit and just listen, it's never less than fun. And fans of ironic pop with a penchant for the cool intelligence of Stereolab or Broadcast, or even Slapp Happy may enjoy.

'A Song In Latin About The Importance Of Comfortable Shoes'

To the untrained ear, Lee could be some breezy Brazilian singer happily intoning over the funky drummer beat with what sounds like some turntablism, stabs of organ, cute bass notes, and random spoken voices. Groovy. But what does it all mean? Who cares! There's a slightly fumbled piano solo and some disco synth.

'A Song In Spanish Addressed To Men Who Drive Big Cars'
There's a funk rhythm and the same effortless vocal style set to sly intelligent party music.

'A Song In Japanese About Trying Things Out Before Committing'
Farty bass sounds, weird 'trumpet' and hilarious synths, as well as piano and shakers, populate this buoyant wee piece of fluff.

'A Song In Bulgarian For Lovers Of Gin'
This piece is cute as anything with its big beats and bicycle bells, dub guitar effects and weird stretching elephant cries, sampled and looped.

'A Song In German Concerning Gardens And Goodbyes'
With its lush 1940s orchestra, bird song, brisk beat, cooing backing singers, and hints of smoky sax, organ and harp, the only barrier to a good time is the German language, which never sounds breezy!

'A Song In Italian Saluting His Mother'
Featuring 1970s blaxploitation grooves, there's a strange contrast between the James Brown-style music and Lee's whiter-than-white, expressionless voice. This is the only song with guest players: a guitar solo by Ollie Harris and a drum loop by Jack Ross.

'A Song In Danish In Which There Is Much Discontent'
The 'discontent' the title refers to is reflected in the instrumental break featuring some godawful noise-maker. Aside from that, there's a slow beat, deep bass, sly funk, with piano and a touch of feedback.

'A Song In Hindi For Insomniacs'
The longest song here at 7:39 features a slow, heavy beat, and possibly a Variophon or a cheap organ, synth farts, and turntable malarkey. Perhaps the oddest thing on the record, it sounds super strange hearing Lee's voice singing in Hindi.

'A Song In Yoruba About Leaves, Memory And Time'
Featuring cute synth arpeggios, piano, tape-manipulated guitar, and slow funk beats, this is a sweet goodbye.

Phill Brown

Allinson/Brown – AV1 (1998)

Personnel:
Marty Alderdice: not specified
Dave Allinson: not specified
John Cope (aka Mark Hollis): piano
Mark Feltham: harmonica
Jon Kirby: not specified
Hamish Laishley: not specified
Produced by Phill Brown at High Green, Circulation, Lingfield House
Released: 30 March 1998
Running time: 51:30

This odd and rather obscure 1998 release was tied in with an art exhibition, and eventually cobbled together for CD release. Despite its odd provenance, however, it somehow fits nicely into the rather meagre world of Talk Talk-related side projects. That's partly because Mark Hollis performs on one piece, but also because the largely ambient project is one of the better examples of its type. Mostly, however, it's due to the atmosphere of the second track, which sports a drum groove that's like an offcut from *Laughing Stock*.

While it's a minor release, its mere existence is intriguing, and any serious collector of Talk Talk-related curios will want to own a copy.

The Talk Talk connections are via engineer Phill Brown, harmonica legend Mark Feltham and Mark Hollis, who, presumably for contractual reasons, is credited here as John Cope. The other credited musicians – including Dave Allinson, Marty Alderdice, Jon Kirby and Hamish Laishley – all appear to be somewhat obscure.

'AV1- Part 1'

This is the longest track by any Talk Talk-related act. Running for an epic 19:25, 'AV1 – Part 1' starts off sounding like many other fairly generic ambient sound artworks. But when the listener sits back and orients themself to the soundworld, it becomes apparent that it's not so different to the parts of 'O'Rang that don't feature drums.

In fact, it could almost be a side project by that group, with its slightly haunted flutes and ghostly sonic apparitions and the odd 'scream' and a touch of the piano from the haunted underwater dance floor of the Titanic. There are bell-like sounds and droning double basses and more.

Like most ambient music, however, it's probably best listened to on headphones, where a concentrated, granular approach can be taken in order to fully appreciate the detail, and hear it above the typical sound floor.

Ambient-oriented music can seem quite dull to the initiate, as there's little in the way of melody to contemplate and it can easily sound like sonic wallpaper. But take a deep breath, wait until late at night when the neighbourhood is quiet, and turn off the lights. You might be surprised.

'AV1 – Part 2'

A mere ten minutes and nine seconds long, 'AV1 – Part 2' gets straight into a pleasantly Talk Talk-cum-O'Rang style drum groove. The guitar is astringent and the drumming could be human or propelled entirely by machines; it resounds nicely in space and there's a certain enjoyable gait and depth and echo to their thwacks.

A careful listen will also reveal electronics, piano and a brief, scratchy pretend-guitar figure.

Towards the end, there are backward elements before the drums finally cease, whereupon you can hear odd sounds and the faint clang of guitar.

'Piano'

The track that everyone wants the *AV1 CD* for, 'Piano', is of course our man, Mark Hollis. Except that, it's really disappointing. The person softly extrapolating on the piano could be anyone, and there's nothing especially interesting about it.

Mark is said to have recorded the piece at his home and then looped it to double the running time to an excessive 14 minutes and 30 seconds. It would be interesting to uncover the logic of that decision, or even whether the looping was his idea.

In the opinion of this fan, 'Piano' is the least interesting track on *AV1*. Pleasant enough, but that's all.

Dedicated collectors should note that the track is also included on the *Missing Pieces* CD of *Laughing Stock* cut-offs compiled on Phill's short-lived Pond Life label. Both *Missing Pieces* and *AV1* are now out of print, however.

'Steel'

The final track is 7:24 in length and features a very *Laughing Stock*, Mark-like guitar, as well as piano and cello. It has a very hushed atmosphere, although not a lot happens.

Brief Mentions

Worthy of brief mentions are a few albums that former members of Talk Talk have played on. One of these is Norwegian band Midnight Choir's rather dark, richly gothic album *Waiting For The Bricks To Fall* (2003, reissued 2019). Lee Harris played drums, Tim Friese-Green arranged the strings and choir, and Phill Brown engineered. Lee also drummed on the very Talk Talk-like 2004 Bark Psychosis album, *Codename: Dustsucker*, and performed alongside his hero, Can drummer Jaki Liebezeit, on Magnetic North's *Evolver* (2012).

The Talk Talk Tributes

Various Artists – **Spirit Of Talk Talk** (2012)

Produced at The Lodge, The Thin Line, Sneaky Studios, Durtin Studio, Trout Recording, RAK Studios, Greenmount Studios, Chevalec Studios, Art Of June Studios, Florence Gardens.

Release date: 3 September 2012.

Running time: 120:16

Released in September 2012 as an 'all proceeds to charity' taster for the *Spirit Of Talk Talk* book, this generous 30-track double CD (with three 'bonus' tracks online) features an international line-up of acts covering songs from the Talk Talk catalogue.

On its release, this tribute received mediocre reviews with a tendency to write off the majority of its interpretations as bringing nothing especially new to the table. Certainly, for a more consistently rewarding set, curator Alan Wilder might have either been bolder in his selection of artists or made a decision to choose more compatible acts, and therefore make it a more immersive listening experience. Certainly, few will have the patience to sit down for its too-long running time (Wilder could have taken note of Talk Talk's own intentionally LP-length albums), instead opting to push 'play' on selected tracks.

(Is Wilder even a Talk Talk fan? He's been quoted as saying of Mark: 'A seemingly more miserable person I couldn't imagine... we would be met with a blank stare whenever we tried to make conversation with him').

Spirit Of Talk Talk could be a lot worse, however, and it's never less than mildly entertaining to hear how miscellaneous groups and artists approach their choice of Talk Talk song.

Disc 1

Lone Wolf – 'Wealth'

Singer-songwriter Lone Wolf, aka Paul Marshall (who was considered up-and-coming in 2012 but has since all but disappeared from the scene) begins his rendition of the *Spirit Of Eden* song with echoed acapella voice, emphasising the devotional feeling of the original with some resonant church-like organ (or simulation thereof). At least this Lone Wolf sounds like he means it.

Zero 7 – 'The Colour Of Spring'

UK duo Zero 7 (Henry Binns and Sam Hardaker) have been responsible for some sophisticated mellow grooves going back to the late 1990s, and like similar electronic/producer-based duos, rely on guest singers. Here they use Only Girl (aka Londoner Ellen Murphy), who renders 'The Colour Of Spring' almost unrecognisable. Radical reinventions can sometimes be wonderful, but Zero 7, on this occasion, can't resist going down the remix/remodel path, backwards-looping Mark's guitar, mucking around with electronic sounds. It's pleasant enough but ...

S. Cary – 'I Believe In You'
Featuring bass, flute, guitar, percussion and electronics, Bon Iver member Sean Carey's attempt at the *Spirit Of Eden* song is faithful, but his high, effortless multitracked vocals – together with a bluesy guitar solo and prominent flute – make it just different enough to sound fresh.

Recoil – 'Dum Dum Girl'
Recoil is the project of former Depeche Mode member Alan Wilder, who is also the curator of *Spirit Of Talk Talk*. His version of the *It's My Life* track is one of the highlights. Featuring David Rhodes (guitar) and Martin Ditcham (percussion), along with diva Shara Nova, Wilder successfully removes the '80s gloss, adding an orchestral-style arrangement that emphasises the mystery of the song construction.

Duncan Sheik – 'Life's What You Make It'
The American singer-songwriter grew up listening to bands like Blue Nile and Talk Talk, and his cover of *The Colour Of Spring* hit is given quite a makeover with mostly acoustic instruments – including hammered dulcimer, acoustic guitar, harmonium and piano – all played by Sheik. The original is, of course, unbeatable, but music's not a competition, and Sheik shows that it's possible to present another side of this song without altering the structure, just its tone and texture.

Thomas Feiner, Fyfe Dangerfield, Robbie Wilson – 'The Rainbow'
This odd collaboration between one Swedish and two UK musician/songwriters is possibly the most ambitious rendering of a Talk Talk song on the album. It begins with a choral section, then a small orchestra fires up before a deep male voice vaguely in the gothic style of Nick Cave interprets the words.

Halloween, Alaska – 'After The Flood'
One of the candidates for worst version of a Talk Talk song, American band Halloween, Alaska seem to be intent on destroying the unique mood of this *Laughing Stock* song. There are sharp, echoing drums, generic vocals, a mindlessly repetitive guitar figure and a 'build' that makes it obvious they want to turn it into some kind of stadium anthem. No, just no!

Nils Frahm, Peter Broderick, David Rossi – 'It's Getting Late In The Evening'
This B-side is an interesting choice and pianist/composer/electronic musician Nils Frahm and his two friends certainly have the skills and the sensibilities to do Talk Talk justice. It starts with a soothing voice (Peter Broderick), piano and

a lush string section. Soon, Broderick's vocals balloon into a choral feature that certainly makes it one of the more unusual tracks, if not the most likeable.

King Creosote – 'Give It Up'
Scottish act King Creosote (aka Kenny Anderson) has an irrepressible personality and that comes through in spades on his um … unique version of the most outwardly soulful song on *The Colour Of Spring*. His rough-cast voice, earthy accordion and acoustic guitar make this one of the stand-out tracks. Does it transcend the original version? Of course not, but at least it's got personality.

Lights – 'Living In Another World'
From one of the better tracks to one of the worst. Lights (Canadian singer Valerie Bokan) collaborates with electronic group Darkstars for this example of plastic pop, 2012-style. Lights sound like a candy-voiced doll, while the stereo-panning audio SFX merely irritates. Just wrong.

Zelienople – 'The Rainbow'
A second version of this great song, but sadly, the Chicago group sound like a bunch of sad sack wannabe Mark Hollises. Matt Christensen tries (but fails) to sing like Mark and his guitar even tries to imitate Mark's. But alas, the result is rather poor.

Joan As Police Woman – 'Myrrhman'
Okay, so it doesn't sound a lot like the 'Myrrhman' we know and love, but at least the eccentric Joan Wasser has the balls to do her own thing and 'own' the song. Anyone familiar with Wasser's work will know what to expect. The result is a bit of an epic at 7:03 and includes a delightfully slowed-down section with intentionally wonky strings and guitar.

The Last Dinosaur – 'Runeii'
The Last Dinosaur, aka Jamie Cameron, a former member of the BMX Bandits, produces and plays every instrument except the violin in his rendition of the *Laughing Stock* song. Unfortunately, Cameron pointedly ignores one of the key points of latter-day Talk Talk: the importance of minimalism. The low-down guitar figure that makes 'Runeii' so distinctive is in evidence, but the potency of the song is watered down by pointless decoration. There are violins and piano and various audio sound effects. It's too much and, therefore, too little. And it's a mess.

Jack Northover – '?'
Another interesting choice and a very different, rather bold take on the song by UK folk singer-songwriter Northover. An old 78rpm record briefly plays and when it fades out, the sound of the needle in the shellac continues while Northover sings in his dulcet tone, with strings and harmonica accompaniment.

The TenFiveSixty – 'It's My Life'
Obscure UK group The TenFiveSixty illustrate why they're not better known with this frankly horrid take on a song that could have been nicely freshened up. Instead, this is plastic power pop and a wasted opportunity.

Disc 2
Recoil – 'Inheritance'
A second track featuring curator Alan Wilder's electronic Recoil project, it's a fascinating, if rather flawed, attempt to do something completely different with the *Spirit Of Eden* track. Featuring the spoken voice of dub poet Linton Kwesi Johnson, the track loses its focus a little when it also adds Paul Marshall's singing. Still, its almost industrial electronic sound and some bass-heavy moments towards the end make it deliciously different.

Turin Brakes – 'Ascension Day'
UK folk-rock group Turin Brakes are one of the more well-known names on *Spirit Of Talk Talk,* and the duo seem to instinctively locate the blues buried deep in 'Ascension Day'. In fact, by the end, they turn it into a chain-gang call-and-response holler, and it works.

White Belt Yellow Tag – 'Today'
British alt-rock band White Belt Yellow Tag, on the other hand, have no idea what to do with this track from Talk Talk's album debut, so they fashion a rendition that emphasises the plastic production of the original rather than dig in to find the quality in the songwriting.

Ian Curnow – 'I Don't Believe In You'
It's surprising and disappointing that Curnow (who was a regular guest keyboardist in Talk Talk and toured with the band) fails to find a compelling reason for covering this great song. The singer, known as Human, is kind of meh, for starters. It doesn't help that the music is too shiny and rather pastel. Why bother? Even the presence of David Rhodes fails to beef it up.

Goldheart Assembly – 'Chameleon Day'
Curnow could learn a thing or two from this English band, whose interpretation of the *Colour Of Spring* song takes liberties and is all the better for it. There are restful multi-tracked vocals, and the background is pleasantly ambient until the song starts to build up a head of steam.

Matthias Vogt Trio – 'April 5th'
Including an acoustic jazz trio on an album of Talk Talk covers might be an odd decision, especially given the fact that the German outfit's version is entirely instrumental. Regardless, this makes for a delightful break from the

various and sundry attempts that make up *Spirit Of Talk Talk*. Mark might have even enjoyed this, because it's suitably spare. And, of course, he loved jazz.

Do Make Say Think – 'New Grass'

This Canadian group are clearly a post-rock outfit influenced by *Spirit Of Eden* and *Laughing Stock,* and a perfect fit for this project. The fact that their version of 'New Grass' sounds more like post-Syd (pre-*Dark Side Of The Moon*) Pink Floyd is beside the point. Fab!

Jason Lytle – 'Tomorrow's Started '

The former leader of acclaimed American group Grandaddy sings well on his interpretation of one of Talk Talk's more date-stamped songs, but he sadly resists the urge to bring the music itself into the 21st century. Still, it's one of the better cuts.

White Lies – 'Give It Up'

A second version of Talk Talk's most obviously soul-influenced song by the London trio White Lies fails to really gel. Harry McVeigh sings in a fruity, theatrical croon that might have worked had the music itself been less synthetic sounding with its glistening keyboard sound and tinny drum machine.

Lia Ices – 'Time It's Time'

The American singer-songwriter multi-tracks her whispery voice-over rather plinkety-plonk synthesizer arpeggiations, which makes it sound more dated than the original version ever will.

The Lovetones – 'The Party's Over'

Australian psychedelic rock band The Lovetones bizarrely choose the title track from Talk Talk's debut album, and while their version is competent, it reveals nothing startlingly new.

Thomas White – 'Candy'

A former member of The Electric Soft Parade, singer-songwriter Thomas White, like The Lovetones, chooses one of Talk Talk's very early songs. White sings like a Las Vegas crooner and the music's initially unpromising. But there is a real progression – and some nice deep bass lines – and by the end, it feels like he's given the old tune a bit of a shake-up.

The Black Ships – 'Renee'

There are plucked strings and an ambient background, but honestly, this US group (and its UK singer Amelia Tucker) fail to transform what is already a plaintive ballad or give us any insight into the song.

The Acorn – 'Taphead'
Canadian group The Acorn sound like they really, really want to be Talk Talk, and they pretty much copy 'Taphead' note for note.

Richard Reed Perry – 'I Believe In You'
Another Canadian singer-songwriter, Arcade Fire's Richard Reed Perry sports a light voice and plays an old piano on this pleasant but unremarkable version.

Note: There are three bonus cuts on streaming services, including Minerva Lions' bluesy version of 'Ascension Day', Mike Gill's really horrible dance mix of 'It's My Life' and Kurran & The Wolfnotes' pointless rendition of 'Eden'.

Held By Trees – Solace (2022)
Personnel:
Eric Bibb: guitar
Simon Edwards: acoustic bass
Mary Apperley: cello
Martin Ditcham: drums, percussion
Steve Smith: organ
Grant Howard: organ, electric piano
Andy Panayi: flute, clarinet
David Knopfler: guitar
Justin Kniest: guitar
Robbie McIntosh: guitar
Tim Renwick: guitar
Chris Mears: bowed guitar
David Joseph: guitar, piano, harmonium, kalimba
Peter Moon: piano
Lawrence Pendrous: piano, harmonium
Mike Smith: saxophone
Gary Alesbrook: trumpet
Oskar Apperley: viola
Tristan Apperley: violin
Produced by David Joseph.
UK release date: 22 April 2022.
Running time: 37.35

Curated by multi-instrumentalist producer-writer David Joseph – previously known by the name David Griffiths as frontman for UK Christian rock band Bosh – Held By Trees' *Solace* is an album heavily inspired by *Spirit Of Eden* and *Laughing Stock* and featuring appearances by musicians from those sessions.
   Joseph says that the idea came about during the Covid-19 pandemic lockdown. With motorways empty and flights cancelled, everything went quiet, and nature was revealed in all its glory.

Much of its appeal derives from the fact that despite Talk Talk's lasting influence on generations of so-called post-rock and 'alternative' rock bands, few have been overt in attempting to create music that traces specifically on the outlines of those two seminal albums. With so few playing minutes of late-period Talk Talk available, it's not surprising that there's an eager market for 'sounds like' product.

Joseph has certainly been canny in roping in a variety of Talk Talk-connected contributors. Engineer Phill Brown, bassist Simon Edwards, percussionist Martin Ditcham, flautist Andy Panayi, guitarist Robbie McIntosh and pianist Lawrence Pendrous all guest on *Solace*, and although James Marsh stopped short of offering one of his artworks, he did design the rather frugal logo.

Somewhat oddly, *Solace* also features guest shots from Dire Straits guitarist David Knopfler (brother of Mark), guitarist Tim Renwick (Pink Floyd, David Bowie), saxist Mike Smith (Blur, Damon Albarn), trumpeter Gary Alesbrook (Noel Gallagher, Kasabian) and blues player Eric Bibb. These musical infusions rather muddy the aesthetic water.

The obvious elephant in the room is the absence of Mark Hollis, or indeed, any singer at all. Mark's vocals are the most recognisable feature and the key sonic characteristic on all the Talk Talk recordings, so the instrumental Held By Trees project is always going to be less intense and nowhere near as emotive. I guess it might have been called Spirit Of Talk Talk if that title hadn't already been taken, but even at its best, *Solace* can only ever aspire to provide an impressionistic patina of familiar patterns, shapes and moods.

Despite its shortcomings, the album has been well-received, and a touring version of Held By Trees is now operative. This is surprising, given the aesthetic transgressions found in its eight songs. *Spirit Of Eden, Laughing Stock* and *Mark Hollis* are famed for the way they value silence, their sometimes extreme dynamics and the way they capture beauty without resorting to cheesy musical cliches. Annoyingly, *Solace* does exactly that with its new age/easy-listening melodies, conventional blues guitar and sleazy sax transgressions. No wonder Paul, Lee and Tim stayed away from this project. Their own projects have so much more to offer.

'Next To Silence'
David Joseph made a bunch of nature recordings for *Solace,* and 'Next To Silence' begins with the sound of birds chirping, joined by reflective piano, flute, harmonium and strings. The hushed ambience of Talk Talk (and the *Mark Hollis* album) is immediately apparent. It's so pretty, however, that it could easily be mistaken for one of those 1980s Windham Hill label new age records.

'In The Trees'
Martin Ditcham supplies the patented Lee Harris beat and there's an atmospheric, heavily reverbed guitar, as well as piano and acoustic bass.

It's lovely, but a short bluesy guitar solo (presumably supplied by Robbie McIntosh) sounds out of place.

'Rain After Sun'
The sound of rain is joined by guitar, piano, drums and – wait for it – a smoky sax that sounds, um ... out of place.

'Wave Upon Wave'
Waves recorded at Bournemouth Beach introduce a piece featuring echoed guitar, piano, acoustic bass and acoustic guitar courtesy of blues player Eric Bibb.

'An Approach'
Slight variations on one long harmonium/organ chord, a few plucked acoustic guitar notes, and that's all.

'The Tree Of Life'
Ditcham's doom-laden drums set the scene for some guitar soloing on both electric and acoustic. Seemingly created as an outlet for Tim Renwick, 'The Tree Of Life' sounds much more of Pink Floyd's sound world than Talk Talk's. As if that wasn't enough to unsettle, there's a short acoustic guitar solo that sounds like it came straight off a cod-classical Sky record. At the end, Gary Alesbrook toots his trumpet pleasantly. This tree doesn't quite hang together.

'Mysterium'
Mark's school teacher pal Lawrence Pendrous performs the piano and harmonium parts on 'Mysterium', over which is draped a hovering orchestral ambience. Robbie McIntosh does the guitar honours. While there are recognisably Talk Talk elements here, melodically, it's something else altogether: cheesy easy listening music that Mark would have baulked at.

'The New Earth'
While the first few tracks on *Solace* are indicative of good intentions, this last track tramples all over that idea and reveals an astonishing lack of insight into the Talk Talk aesthetic. There's another sustained orchestral chord under which there's a piano figure straight out of some TV show theme. Again, there's no edge, which takes it straight into new age/easy listening territory. Then (horror of horrors) it goes into an awful happy gallop full of electric guitar flatulence (McIntosh again) and sloppy seconds from Mike Smith's sleazy sax.

The Talk Talk Legacy

The story of Talk Talk is like no other in the annals of pop music, though certain strands have parallels with other groups. For instance, Japan went through a similarly swift evolution, but instead of making era-defining albums, they broke up, leaving singer David Sylvian to follow a very different but equally self-defined and exploratory road to that of Mark Hollis.

It's frustrating that so little is known about the private Mark Hollis, but also gratifying. Looking at the obscene end of the celebrity spectrum, we see how a figure like hip-hop colossus Kanye West has become so notorious for his bizarre behaviour that it's almost impossible to focus on any musical worth he might have. Mark, by all accounts, lived a quiet, family-oriented life, but small anecdotes from music collaborators show that he did have a sharp and sometimes cruel sense of humour, that he could be generous (and mean) and that one of his favourite pursuits was to sit quaffing beer in crowded pubs, usually in silence.

That information rather breaks the spell of the very reverent Talk Talk. Personally, I'm happy just to have the music. We're naturally curious about Hollis and his various collaborators, but it gives us nothing that we didn't already have when the music cast its spell.

The group's influence on contemporary rock music is incalculable. The whole so-called post-rock genre grew from the seeds planted by *Spirit Of Eden* and *Laughing Stock,* and then there are those bands whose music cleaves much closer to the sound of Talk Talk: those who aren't just influenced or inspired by them but have created music almost in their image. One of these is Bark Psychosis, whose *Hex* (1994) album bares many of the hallmarks from the gently reverbed guitars to the sudden outbreaks of dynamics into a fury around which there are lakes and glaciers of calm and beauty. The leader of Bark Psychosis, Graham Sutton, was one of the large cast of the 'O'Rang albums and Lee returned the favour by giving good advice for *Hex* and contributing majorly to the next Bark Psychosis album. While Graham's not a naturally gifted blue-eyed soul singer like Mark and instead uses his pleasant voice to more or less 'talk in tune' like so many English singers (The The's Matt Johnson being a good case in point... and he appeared on the first 'O'Rang album!) Sutton does play a mean guitar, and anything he's involved in tends to sound wonderful from an engineering point of view.

There are too many bands heavily in debt to the spirit of Talk Talk to mention them all, but it would be remiss not to mention Elbow, who have crafted a much more middle-of-the-road, accessible take on the formula. It could be said that they've taken some of the gentrified, song-oriented sound and textures from *The Colour Of Spring* and added a few textures and some of the hushed ambience of the last two without getting into the extremities of those records.

These New Puritans are a much more obvious Talk Talk-influenced group and it could be said that they've taken the experiments of the last two Talk

Talk albums as well as the orchestral elements of the Mark Hollis album to create their extremely intimate and exacting musical universe. The 2013 album *Fields Of Reeds,* especially, can't be said to intentionally emulate Talk Talk, but the exquisite textures, dynamics and hushed beauty of the album make it an especially notable kissing cousin.

But perhaps the real Talk Talk legacy is with the fans, who now know what it's like to experience transcendence through music, and a sense of the tremendous joy and sorrow that's all part and parcel of the human experience.

On Track series

Allman Brothers Band – Andrew Wild 978-1-78952-252-5
Tori Amos – Lisa Torem 978-1-78952-142-9
Aphex Twin – Beau Waddell 978-1-78952-267-9
Asia – Peter Braidis 978-1-78952-099-6
Badfinger – Robert Day-Webb 978-1-878952-176-4
Barclay James Harvest – Keith and Monica Domone 978-1-78952-067-5
Beck – Arthur Lizie 978-1-78952-258-7
The Beatles – Andrew Wild 978-1-78952-009-5
The Beatles Solo 1969-1980 – Andrew Wild 978-1-78952-030-9
Blue Oyster Cult – Jacob Holm-Lupo 978-1-78952-007-1
Blur – Matt Bishop 978-178952-164-1
Marc Bolan and T.Rex – Peter Gallagher 978-1-78952-124-5
Kate Bush – Bill Thomas 978-1-78952-097-2
Camel – Hamish Kuzminski 978-1-78952-040-8
Captain Beefheart – Opher Goodwin 978-1-78952-235-8
Caravan – Andy Boot 978-1-78952-127-6
Cardiacs – Eric Benac 978-1-78952-131-3
Nick Cave and The Bad Seeds – Dominic Sanderson 978-1-78952-240-2
Eric Clapton Solo – Andrew Wild 978-1-78952-141-2
The Clash – Nick Assirati 978-1-78952-077-4
Elvis Costello and The Attractions – Georg Purvis 978-1-78952-129-0
Crosby, Stills and Nash – Andrew Wild 978-1-78952-039-2
Creedence Clearwater Revival – Tony Thompson 978-178952-237-2
The Damned – Morgan Brown 978-1-78952-136-8
Deep Purple and Rainbow 1968-79 – Steve Pilkington 978-1-78952-002-6
Dire Straits – Andrew Wild 978-1-78952-044-6
The Doors – Tony Thompson 978-1-78952-137-5
Dream Theater – Jordan Blum 978-1-78952-050-7
Eagles – John Van der Kiste 978-1-78952-260-0
Earth, Wind and Fire – Bud Wilkins 978-1-78952-272-3
Electric Light Orchestra – Barry Delve 978-1-78952-152-8
Emerson Lake and Palmer – Mike Goode 978-1-78952-000-2
Fairport Convention – Kevan Furbank 978-1-78952-051-4
Peter Gabriel – Graeme Scarfe 978-1-78952-138-2
Genesis – Stuart MacFarlane 978-1-78952-005-7
Gentle Giant – Gary Steel 978-1-78952-058-3
Gong – Kevan Furbank 978-1-78952-082-8
Green Day – William E. Spevack 978-1-78952-261-7
Hall and Oates – Ian Abrahams 978-1-78952-167-2
Hawkwind – Duncan Harris 978-1-78952-052-1
Peter Hammill – Richard Rees Jones 978-1-78952-163-4
Roy Harper – Opher Goodwin 978-1-78952-130-6

Jimi Hendrix – Emma Stott 978-1-78952-175-7
The Hollies – Andrew Darlington 978-1-78952-159-7
Horslips – Richard James 978-1-78952-263-1
The Human League and The Sheffield Scene –
Andrew Darlington 978-1-78952-186-3
The Incredible String Band – Tim Moon 978-1-78952-107-8
Iron Maiden – Steve Pilkington 978-1-78952-061-3
Joe Jackson – Richard James 978-1-78952-189-4
Jefferson Airplane – Richard Butterworth 978-1-78952-143-6
Jethro Tull – Jordan Blum 978-1-78952-016-3
Elton John in the 1970s – Peter Kearns 978-1-78952-034-7
Billy Joel – Lisa Torem 978-1-78952-183-2
Judas Priest – John Tucker 978-1-78952-018-7
Kansas – Kevin Cummings 978-1-78952-057-6
The Kinks – Martin Hutchinson 978-1-78952-172-6
Korn – Matt Karpe 978-1-78952-153-5
Led Zeppelin – Steve Pilkington 978-1-78952-151-1
Level 42 – Matt Philips 978-1-78952-102-3
Little Feat – Georg Purvis - 978-1-78952-168-9
Aimee Mann – Jez Rowden 978-1-78952-036-1
Joni Mitchell – Peter Kearns 978-1-78952-081-1
The Moody Blues – Geoffrey Feakes 978-1-78952-042-2
Motorhead – Duncan Harris 978-1-78952-173-3
Nektar – Scott Meze – 978-1-78952-257-0
New Order – Dennis Remmer – 978-1-78952-249-5
Nightwish – Simon McMurdo – 978-1-78952-270-9
Laura Nyro – Philip Ward 978-1-78952-182-5
Mike Oldfield – Ryan Yard 978-1-78952-060-6
Opeth – Jordan Blum 978-1-78-952-166-5
Pearl Jam – Ben L. Connor 978-1-78952-188-7
Tom Petty – Richard James 978-1-78952-128-3
Pink Floyd – Richard Butterworth 978-1-78952-242-6
The Police – Pete Braidis 978-1-78952-158-0
Porcupine Tree – Nick Holmes 978-1-78952-144-3
Queen – Andrew Wild 978-1-78952-003-3
Radiohead – William Allen 978-1-78952-149-8
Rancid – Paul Matts 989-1-78952-187-0
Renaissance – David Detmer 978-1-78952-062-0
REO Speedwagon – Jim Romag 978-1-78952-262-4
The Rolling Stones 1963-80 – Steve Pilkington 978-1-78952-017-0
The Smiths and Morrissey – Tommy Gunnarsson 978-1-78952-140-5
Spirit – Rev. Keith A. Gordon – 978-1-78952- 248-8
Stackridge – Alan Draper 978-1-78952-232-7

Pink Floyd In The 1970s – Georg Purvis 978-1-78952-072-9
Suzi Quatro in the 1970s – Darren Johnson 978-1-78952-236-5
Queen in the 1970s – James Griffiths 978-1-78952-265-5
Roxy Music in the 1970s – Dave Thompson 978-1-78952-180-1
Slade in the 1970s – Darren Johnson 978-1-78952-268-6
Status Quo in the 1980s – Greg Harper 978-1-78952-244-0
Tangerine Dream in the 1970s – Stephen Palmer 978-1-78952-161-0
The Sweet in the 1970s – Darren Johnson 978-1-78952-139-9
Uriah Heep in the 1970s – Steve Pilkington 978-1-78952-103-0
Van der Graaf Generator in the 1970s – Steve Pilkington 978-1-78952-245-7
Rick Wakeman in the 1970s – Geoffrey Feakes 978-1-78952-264-8
Yes in the 1980s – Stephen Lambe with David Watkinson 978-1-78952-125-2

On Screen series
Carry On… – Stephen Lambe 978-1-78952-004-0
David Cronenberg – Patrick Chapman 978-1-78952-071-2
Doctor Who: The David Tennant Years – Jamie Hailstone 978-1-78952-066-8
James Bond – Andrew Wild 978-1-78952-010-1
Monty Python – Steve Pilkington 978-1-78952-047-7
Seinfeld Seasons 1 to 5 – Stephen Lambe 978-1-78952-012-5

Other Books
1967: A Year In Psychedelic Rock 978-1-78952-155-9
1970: A Year In Rock – John Van der Kiste 978-1-78952-147-4
1973: The Golden Year of Progressive Rock 978-1-78952-165-8
Babysitting A Band On The Rocks – G.D. Praetorius 978-1-78952-106-1
Eric Clapton Sessions – Andrew Wild 978-1-78952-177-1
Derek Taylor: For Your Radioactive Children –
Andrew Darlington 978-1-78952-038-5
The Golden Road: The Recording History of The Grateful Dead – John
Kilbride 978-1-78952-156-6
Iggy and The Stooges On Stage 1967-1974 – Per Nilsen 978-1-78952-101-6
Jon Anderson and the Warriors – the road to Yes –
David Watkinson 978-1-78952-059-0
Magic: The David Paton Story – David Paton 978-1-78952-266-2
Misty: The Music of Johnny Mathis – Jakob Baekgaard 978-1-78952-247-1
Nu Metal: A Definitive Guide – Matt Karpe 978-1-78952-063-7
Tommy Bolin: In and Out of Deep Purple – Laura Shenton 978-1-78952-070-5
Maximum Darkness – Deke Leonard 978-1-78952-048-4
The Twang Dynasty – Deke Leonard 978-1-78952-049-1

and many more to come!

Would you like to write for Sonicbond Publishing?

At Sonicbond Publishing we are always on the look-out for authors, particularly for our two main series:

On Track. Mixing fact with in depth analysis, the On Track series examines the work of a particular musical artist or group. All genres are considered from easy listening and jazz to 60s soul to 90s pop, via rock and metal.

On Screen. This series looks at the world of film and television. Subjects considered include directors, actors and writers, as well as entire television and film series. As with the On Track series, we balance fact with analysis.

While professional writing experience would, of course, be an advantage the most important qualification is to have real enthusiasm and knowledge of your subject. First-time authors are welcomed, but the ability to write well in English is essential.

Sonicbond Publishing has distribution throughout Europe and North America, and all books are also published in E-book form. Authors will be paid a royalty based on sales of their book.

Further details are available from www.sonicbondpublishing.co.uk. To contact us, complete the contact form there or email info@sonicbondpublishing.co.uk